Letters to an Unknown Generation

Books by DAVID G. YUENGLING

Letters to an Unknown Generation
Highlights in the Debates in the Spanish Chamber of
Deputies Relative to the Abandonment of Santo Domingo

LETTERS TO AN UNKNOWN GENERATION

by

DAVID G. YUENGLING

Exposition Press   Hicksville, New York

FIRST EDITION

© 1979 by David G. Yuengling

ISBN 0-682-49389-9

Printed in the United States of America

To
Dick and Bobbie
and
Bob and Angela

Contents

A Letter to the Unknown Generations in My Family

To those of you who will succeed my generation, I extend greetings. It seems somewhat strange for me to be writing a letter to you who are, or will be, members of future generations of the Yuengling family. But write to you I must, because I feel that I, as a member of my own generation, have something to give to you which, as you grow up and when you become of age, you may find to be of some value. I trust this will be the case.

It is nothing tangible I have to offer you but, rather, the intangible of a way of life into which I was born and brought up, and the principles by which I have tried to live. These and the beliefs I espouse all are apparent in the correspondence I have conducted with my family, friends, and acquaintances—a small part of which I have included within these pages.

There is a reason why. Each individual (and this includes every one of you) must, while he is here, live his life in such a way that he will be able to establish a reason for living, a *raison d'être*. This is important because unless one does this there is really no reason for him to be living at all. Life must have meaning, and a man's life must be worthwhile not only to him who lives it but to others as well. Your life should be lived in such a way that the world will be regarded by others as a better place for your having been here.

There are opinions expressed within these pages with which you will agree, and there are other opinions expressed with which you will disagree. That is inevitable. But each of you has been blessed with a culture and a tradition that extend back to remote ancestors of whom you are only dimly aware. The way you will confront the culture and traditions of your background and the social manners and mores of your time will depend upon how much attention you pay to them, and upon the manner in which your parents have brought you up. It is quite possible that within these pages you may find something that will be of service to you.

I have already gone beyond the threescore years ordinarily allotted to man on this planet, and like all of you, I have not been made aware of how much time I will be permitted to remain here. This small volume represents, in part, an expression of my *raison d'être* together with the knowledge and experience it has been my sometime and somewhat painful pleasure to accumulate over this period of years. This I present to you as my legacy. This I leave to you as my heritage.

DAVID G. YUENGLING

An Autobiographical Sketch

Several generations have been born and brought up since my own came into being. The Winds of Time have blown inexorably in one direction and then another, and change has been paramount. The world that was in 1915 is vastly different from the world of the 1970's, and even though an immense holocaust was in progress on the continent of Europe at that time, change, as we know it today, had not yet come to American shores. America, then, was still partly Victorian, but mostly Edwardian in manners and morals.

My parents were typical of that generation. They were fairly well off, and my father had built for my mother a three-storied, old English Tudor-type mansion with spreading lawns and a lovely sunken formal garden that was my mother's pride and joy. For them, 1915 was a year of surprises. They found out they were going to have an addition to their already growing family, and like most post-Edwardian families of America's upper middle class of those days, they sat back and waited. On the morning of July 16 my twin brother and I saw the light of day for the first time.

Twins, I know, were definitely not what my father had had in mind, and while I do not feel that he was too displeased with the result, I have often thought that since I arrived last, I might have arrived more or less as an afterthought. Be that as it may, we were both accepted as members of the household in good standing, and I am sure my mother and father lavished their affection upon me as much as upon my other brothers and sister who had preceded me into this world. It was thus to the tune of bitter squalling and the strict discipline of a German nurse that my twin brother, Dick, and I eventually grew into boyhood.

We were a rather rough-and-tumble group, my brothers and

sister and I, whose main preoccupation during these primary years seemed to be tussling or fighting on the hall or living-room floor; and in matters of skulduggery, since I was the youngest, I was far and away the most eligible to act as the innocent front man for their Machiavellian deeds. In my youth I had always found it difficult to understand why my father stayed so long at his office and took so many business trips to New York and to Philadelphia and why my mother developed the habit of periodically going upstairs to her room and locking herself in the bathroom. But as early youth passed, despite its toll, and I began to grow up, I did receive some inkling as to the reason. They couldn't stand us; that's why. Later in life I knew the reason for certain when my nephews and nieces, fond children of my now-married brothers and sister, began congregating at my parents' home for Sunday dinner and racing each other through the hall, living room, and den during cocktails, whooping it up like a tribe of wild Indians amid such fond parental blandishments as, "Get out of here and play outside. You're disturbing your grandfather."

A brood of five can be a handful for any mother and father, particularly if they happen to be as energetic and adept at thinking up mischief as we were. We were no exception to that rule. It isn't surprising, therefore, that my father and mother had two nurses for their infant gangsters; one for Dohrman, who was my older brother, and one for Dick and myself. I haven't the remotest idea what it was that gave my parents the notion that Dohrman was any less of a terror or scourge of the neighborhood than Dick and I, but that seemed to be the general opinion, at least at home. In the general area of our block the neighbors seemed to have a slightly different point of view, but this didn't always reach my parents' ears.

Being older than the three of us, my oldest brother, Frederick, and my sister, Augusta, didn't need a nurse, and that, to me, appeared strange. Neither one of them was immune from concocting some of the nefarious schemes that, inevitably, resulted in one or more of us being punished or going through agonies of torture by not being permitted to go to the Majestic Theater to see the various chapters of the Daniel Boone serial that would run consecutively each Saturday afternoon. That theater belied its name. It was anything but majestic. It had a rather shady repute, and we were forbidden to go there except when there was something special on the screen. We used to call it the Bucket of Blood. The Daniel Boone serial was considered sufficiently special to make the theater appear adequately respectable for that Saturday afternoon showing.

My father's and mother's idea of an afternoon showing and ours was often a point in dispute. Those were the days before double features, and to them an afternoon showing consisted in going to the theater, seeing the show, and leaving at the point where they came in. Our ideas were far more ingenious and imaginative. To us an afternoon showing consisted in seeing the picture at least three or four times or until we got bored. The result was not always pleasant, nor did we receive thunderous applause when we got home; and what thunderous applause we did receive was, generally, to the tune of the business end of a hairbrush. In those days my parents had never heard of child psychology and didn't realize that whenever we committed a nefarious deed it was entirely their fault. They held the old-fashioned belief that when a child did something wrong he should be punished for it.

As I look back on them now, the years of my childhood were quite happy years, but at the time they appeared to be filled with every kind of imaginable frustration. Dick and I were in the same grade and class in school until we entered college. The first eight years saw us through grammar school and then, since it was more or less a tradition in our family, we were packed off to The Hill. Although my father had been graduated from Andover and had attended The Hill School first, he thought each of his sons should go to The Hill too. I didn't have anything to say about it, but then, it never occurred to me to say anything. My father had gone there, Frederick had attended it, too, Dohrman was already there and in the Fourth Form, Augusta had come and gone from Westover, and it seemed to me a logical sequence of events that Dick and I should attend The Hill School too. We both accepted the decision without question.

The Hill School was and is located in a vague southeasterly direction from our home in Pottsville, Pennsylvania. I have always felt we were sent there rather than to Andover because of the location. In my day it was a strict school with high scholastic standards, and to the best of my knowledge, it still is. But so far as scholastic endeavors were concerned, I have always been grateful to Dohrman. By this time I had had plenty of experience at being the "fall guy" for my brothers, but Dohrman was the one, by reason of age and position as second son, who was destined to take the rap for Dick and me in conditioning Dad and Mother into what they might expect in the matter of grades.

Frederick had been the brain in our family. When he went to The Hill his report card was sent home bristling with A's and Dad and Mother were well pleased. Then Dohrman entered. It was well for him that sixty miles separated our home from the school, but the inevitable result, while suspended for the time being, never failed to materialize once he returned on vacation. Then he would always be called on the carpet because Dad and Mother would constantly be comparing his C's and D's with Frederick's A's. It was always a bright day when Dohrman could point out a B in his defense. Dohrman always knew he was going to pass, and he never failed to so inform Dad and Mother, who, in the light of past experience, gradually developed a "wait and see" attitude, not only with Dohrman but with Dick and me as well. Then, when the blow would fall, Dohrman would utter his anguished cries of "They gypped me!"

All of this, of course, helped Dick and me no end, for by the time we entered The Hill Dad and Mother had become conditioned and even considered themselves lucky to find a C on our report cards. Not one of the three of us ever let our parents down after Dohrman had conditioned them as to what to expect from us, although none of us ever achieved the heights that Frederick had reached.

Dohrman and Dick were athletically inclined. Dohrman co-captained the baseball team and was on the football team, and Dick was a member of the track team and the boxing team. It was largely due to the blandishments of both Dohrman and Dick that I took up boxing and entered the intramural boxing tournament. Both of my brothers felt I couldn't beat my way out of a paper bag and entering the intramural boxing tournament certainly proved it. I didn't win a single fight. But I discovered something. I discovered that boxing can be a lot of fun, and I developed an interest in the sport that has continued to the present day. In the main, though, my interests led me into the field of public speaking, where I managed to excel in some small degree while my brothers were winning their letters in the more glamorous fields of football, baseball, and track.

It was at The Hill, I think, that I reached the decision that led me to enter the School of Foreign Service at Georgetown University. Even as a small child I was deeply interested in politics and in foreign affairs, and I felt I would like to prepare myself to enter the diplomatic service of my country. From what I was able to ascertain. Georgetown was the only school that seemed to have a sufficiently adequate course. My graduation from The Hill had not exactly been with honors, so I entered Georgetown University on final scholastic probation. This was removed at the end of the spring semester, and during my stay at the School of Foreign Service I found that that was to be the pattern of my scholastic existence—final scholastic probation during the fall semesters and an accepted and acceptable student during the spring semesters.

Five critical years passed during this period of training, years whose summers I spent in Italy studying the Italian language, observing the Mussolini regime, and moving warily through England and France, Italy, Yugoslavia, and Albania. Those years were significant years because I began to think with greater seriousness than previously. They were years of breathless expectancy, too, as Hitler marched into a demilitarized Rhineland; as Englebert Dolfuss lay murdered in the Vienna Chancellory and the German war machine swept over defenseless Austria; as Munich reaped the bitter fruit of tragic appeasement; and as Mussolini seized the neighboring Kingdom of Albania and played havoc with the Empire of Ethiopia. These were the years of a prelude.

When war began in September of 1939 I had returned from

the island of Santo Domingo to my classroom at Georgetown University. I had been engaged in research work on that Caribbean island in order to complete a dissertation required for graduation. The news, even though expected, was to my young mind enshrouded in an aura of exciting bewilderment, and my friends and I, educated during the pacifistic thirties, were realistic enough to wonder how soon it would be before we too would be involved in the struggle.

But the time was not yet, for graduation came in 1940, and soon thereafter I and five of my college friends boarded the S.S. *Evangeline,* which was to take us to the island of Trinidad, where we were to serve as civilian auditors for the United States Navy in the construction of the U.S. Naval Air Station. It was both interesting and enjoyable because we came into contact with all sorts and conditions of men, and although I was working twelve and thirteen hours a day, I found myself wrapped in a realism of preparation for war. Then suddenly, and out of nowhere, war struck.

Although we had been expecting it, the majority of us received the news in devastating surprise, and we stood around our radios listening to the reports in stunned silence and with gradually mounting anger. But there was nothing any of us could do. We read and heard about the vast numbers of men, angry, just like ourselves, who were standing in long lines before the offices of enlistment stations throughout the United States, and each of us eventually returned to our country with the intention of entering some branch of the service.

For me events very soon crystallized themselves. I had returned to the United States somewhat weak and rundown as a result of a rather demanding work schedule, and after I was sufficiently recuperated I departed for California, where I entered the Pacific theater of the war as an officer in the United States Merchant Marine. For a time there was a period of training at St. Petersburg, Florida, and at Sheepshead Bay in New York. My travels took me into the South Pacific and finally, when the war was over, into Japan itself. But in a way those were endless days without number, and at sea I began to consider what it was I wanted to do with my life. I was able to reach a conclusion.

My hobby has always been historical research and collecting documentary histories. Since the war I have been advised that I have amassed one of the finest private collections of documentary history in the Commonwealth of Pennsylvania, and since I came to live in Arizona, I have been told that it is (or was at the time of this writing) one of the finest private collections in Arizona. When the war ended and I found myself in Manila Harbor, I decided to combine my hobby with a profession and engage in teaching history at some college or university.

My ship, the S.S. *Benjamin Bonneville*, reached the United States via Japan on December 15, 1945, and following my discharge from the ship, I returned to Pennsylvania, where at the commencement of the second school semester of 1946 I entered the Graduate School of the Univesrity of Pennsylvania to study for my degree of Master of Arts in History. I did not obtain it in one year. Indeed, during the school year of 1946—47 I taught American history and European history at the Admiral Billard Academy in New London, Connecticut. Then I returned to the University of Pennsylvania and obtained my degree in June of 1948.

In the meantime the growing threat of the Communist conspiracy was fast engulfing the world, and in my own country a lazy apathy toward the question seemed to prevail. I don't know when the subject first took hold of me; I believe it was at the Admiral Billard Academy, because it was there that I began to do research into Communist infiltration into the United States, for a series of lectures to the student body. What I learned amazed me, and as time progressed, I gave myself over to the subject and became more and more engrossed in it. The summer of 1947 saw me in Europe watching and observing. In Madrid I had a number of conversations with some very brilliant Spanish gentlemen. Flying to Rome, I was able to catch a glimpse of Communism in action there, and in Athens I saw a nation in the throes of civil war.

But Communism was not the only thing about which I had to worry. My personal life was rather haphazard, and I was a very confused and bewildered young man. Something had happened, something that made me fight back with a bitter resentment, but what it was I am not completely certain.

In the long years of my travels I had always made it a point to attend the church of my faith because here I felt at home. But outside of the confines of my faith I felt I was being hounded and pursued, not by any person or persons, but by a relentless, spiritual entity that I could not understand or fathom. Thus, not knowing from whom or what I was running, I wandered across the world, and I ran. All through the years that encompassed time and space, through Athens, Rome, London, Madrid, Lisbon, and the cities of my own country, I ran until I arrived in Phoenix, Arizona. Here I stopped and faced my pursuer and discovered who it was. I knew now that I could never run away, and wherever I would go, through time and eternity, He would be there also. I was not happy about it. I was decidedly unhappy because I wanted to lead my own life in my own way. It was then that I ceased fighting that particular battle. Irreverently I turned to my God and I said: "All right! All right! You've got me. Now get off my back!"

I know that He is still there, but since that decision was made I no longer feel I am being pursued, and I have experienced an inner calm I had not previously known.

Part I

RELIGION AND MORALITY

The friendships and acquaintances one makes in a lifetime are, in many ways, diverse. In each of them similar goals can be found, but the paths along which they travel to attain their goals are as opposite and as complex as are the personalities of the individuals themselves.

The first two letters that follow are a case in point. The first was addressed to a young German seminary student in Berlin. The second was addressed to a rather confused young American boy who was studying in a religious commune somewhere in Colorado. Both boys are sincere and conscientious. Both have been following different paths to their goals.

April 26, 1964

I was most happy to receive your letter of a few weeks ago and to get a clearer view of the work in which you are engaged. To say the least, it is intensive.

You are correct in your viewpoint and desire that everyone should love God. That goes without saying, but I am sure that God cannot be forced upon any man, and those who are not already convinced of Him can only be approached by gentle persuasion. I think Christ would be the very last person to accept the conversion of an individual who achieved his conversion through emotion or argument. These conversions have a tendency to lapse after the minister or the priest is no longer by one's side. The true conversion must come from a blind faith in the existence of God and/or a divine revelation from within. If the revelation exists within the individual but is lying dormant, then it is the function of the priest or minister to ignite it. In most cases I would judge that a man must have an inbred faith in God before he can experience the revelation of God.

There are many millions, even within the Christian religion, who are atheistically inclined or, because of the temper of the times, are "doubting Thomases." This is indeed a tragedy, because these people possess no spiritual goals, nor can they until they are willing to acknowledge the supremacy of a Supreme Being. While it should be your objective to use your arts of gentle persuasion, this persuasion will accomplish but little unless you are able to kindle the spark of revelation that should exist in each. Yours is going to be a frustrating, soul-racking experience in the work which lies ahead of you. Christ Himself gave warning of this. But there are compensations, and these compensations will more than make up for the frustrations you will have to undergo.

One thing you might bear in mind is this: that a man who intends to make theology his profession for the rest of his life, should study not only the Christian religion but the religions of all men, for in each one, whether it be Christianity, Buddhism, Islam, Confucionism, or whatever, there is good in each of them. In this way you can become knowledgeable of the religions of the world, and this knowledge will give added force to your understanding of man's vision of Heaven, his pursuit of God, and of God's pursuit of man.

November 24, 1971

Dear Michael:

Your letter arrived this morning. Just a few minutes ago I talked on the telephone with the B. B. Kirk Bible Company in Indianapolis, and I asked them to send a dozen Bibles to you and to send me the bill. I imagine the bill will arrive before you get your Bibles because the company will want its money first.

Instead of saying, "Oh, you can buy them at any bookstore," if you had told me the name of the publisher when I first asked for it you would have had your Bibles that much sooner. But, no! You had to fool around and send me a lot of useless information which I didn't want and which I knew anyway. The next time you want anything please answer my questions first. The Bibles are very expensive, so you and your friends take very good care of them.

I read with great interest the newsletter you enclosed. I have a better idea now of what you are doing than I had previously. I don't know if I fully approve of your communal way of living during this preparatory study in which you are engaged for your work in giving yourself to God. This, however, is strictly your business.

Actually, there is really very little difference between you and your Roman Catholic counterpart who would reside in a monastery. The life you have chosen for yourself does, indeed, require a great deal of discipline, and the idea of giving up all worldly possessions and sharing all things in common is fine for someone like yourself. You haven't anything to begin with anyway. I wonder if you would have had the stamina to do this if you had had, shall we say, an income of five hundred or more dollars a month and many of the articles that money would buy. Would you have been willing to turn all of this over to a religious commune just to live and study there? Some people would, but would you?

It is an interesting question. Of course, you don't have that income nor do you have the possessions such an income would buy. Therefore, the question is purely academic. But it would be interesting for you to examine yourself and give that question some thought.

Since this religious commune of yours is in being, there must be some among you who have surrendered their possessions to follow the ideal you profess. I do not know what you call the leader of your colony, but I am sure you must have one. In a Catholic monastery he would be known as an abbot. Let us call the leader of your colony that for the time being.

What actually is happening is that each member of your colony is turning all of his possessions over to your abbot for use for the benefit of the members of the colony. This abbot has to be a pretty savvy guy, business-wise, because he has to support the whole colony of you. He has to buy food at the cheapest price he can get it; he has to run that lodge of yours; he has to sell whatever it is you produce; he has to clothe you and bed you. In short, not only does he have to be a disciplinarian whenever you get out of line, but he has to be a man dedicated to his beliefs while, at the same time, having his feet on the ground.

You may be interested to know that the Christians of the early church at Antioch tried this communal way of living you're experiencing right now. It didn't work. In fact, it got so bad that they had to appeal to the early Christians in Jerusalem to bail them out, and the Jerusalem Christians were dirt poor.

I have no quarrel with your wanting to live a Christian life and to follow your God along whatever path you feel you should. I believe, in principle, in what you and your friends are trying to accomplish, but, dammit, Michael, you are in this world and, physically, you are of this world, and you should contribute to the well-being of this world, not only spiritually but economically too. If you do not contribute to your colony economically, then all you are doing is being a religious parasite, because it is somebody else's financial contribution that is supporting you. Think about that for a while.

February 17, 1976

Dear Maureen:

The past few days have been trying ones because I have been engaged in correspondence quite extensively. And that can be exhausting. The other day I was trying to express some thoughts on paper. It was one of those times when thoughts are very difficult to come by. I looked at the blank sheet of paper in my typewriter and said, "To Hell with it!" and went out to my favorite cocktail lounge for a glass of beer and a game of pool.

You probably would never believe it, but there at El Sombrero, I got into a discussion with one of my pool hustling friends. There is no question about it. The fellow is a pronounced atheist. I was scandalized. Nor did he relieve my mind at all by telling me that he is a follower of the cult who believe that God is dead.

Such an idea is blasphemy, and I believe that those who profess it are so entangled in the web of their own theology they are unable to ascertain a simple truth.

It is inconceivable to me that anyone, looking into the heavens and seeing the order that exists in the universe, can deny the existence of God. Material man of today's generation needs the Hand of God upon him more now than at any time in his history. He is forgetting the social mores which gave the breath of life to individual conscience and so developed the rules of conduct for society. And in doing this he is coming to the false knowledge not that God created man in His own image but that man created God in his. To many people this may be a subconscious or latent knowledge or revelation. But these people who, subconsciously, believe that man created God are the same people who, three thousand years ago, worshipped the golden calf while Moses was on Sinai. In today's age it is these very same people who say that God is dead.

This is very logical because if man created God, then what else can He be but dead? If you can create what you worship, you can also destroy what you worship. What comfort or inspiration, then, can a god whom man has created be to man? Such a god would have to die, and when he does, man becomes empty. There can be no inspiration in such a god because man himself would be the creator and the inspirer.

And this, I fear, is happening to too great an extent. Man is setting himself up above God, as God's creator. It is apparent not only in the "God is dead" cult but also in the astonishing fact that of all the nations of the earth there are only two that forbid the mention of the name of God in the classrooms of their schools. One is the Soviet Union and the other is the United States of America. Appalling, isn't it? Think on that for a while.

March 5, 1977

Dear Betty:

I had not known until recently that you are in Mexico taking Laetril treatments. Fritzie told me of this, and she also told me how seriously ill you are. For this I grieve, because no one enjoys pain or illness of any kind. Having had a brother and two dear friends who were afflicted with the same disease I can readily believe how Bob and Gene must feel, and my heart goes out to them, and to you too.

I hardly know what to say. In one way or another, and at one time or another, we all suffer, whether through our own infirmities and mistakes or through those of others near and dear to us. This is a part of life, and it is required of all of us while we are here. But I believe from my own life this much have I learned: that from the suffering and despair we have endured we gain a quiet dignity; that in the tumult of our lives we learn, and, in learning, we grow. We grow in dignity and in strength of mind and purpose, and, in so doing, we rise above ourselves and make our peace with God.

Wherever you are, my dear, my love goes with you always.

January 16, 1952

Dear Jean:

It was good to receive your letter. I was particularly happy to receive it for several reasons. I had known Robert was dissatisfied with his present or past position in Cleveland, but I didn't know why. Your letter has made things a bit clearer, but I still don't know the story. I am very glad that, whatever it was, it has been cleared up to Robert's satisfaction.

While I was there at Christmas I was, and still am, under the impression there is no place Robert could do so much good or be so worthwhile as he has been and is in Cleveland. I know I am a relative newcomer into your lives, and in all probability I do not know your situation sufficiently well to warrant my speaking.

But I remember one evening after you had gone to bed and Robert and I were sitting downstairs engaged in conversation. He had advised me that the parish was now built up to the point where he felt he could no longer constructively contribute to its harmonious function; that he felt it was time to leave and accept a call from another church; that his successor would step into a fine-running organization without the trials and misgivings he had had to face when he first came there. Those are not the exact words but that in brief was the gist of the conversation.

I was hesitant to express my disagreement. Robert is older than I am and his knowledge is far superior to mine, but I did feel that in that particular instance he was making a grievous error, that in the profession he has chosen, just as, indeed, in that which I have chosen, no man can serve two masters. That night, talking with Robert, I received the impression he was more interested in serving himself than in serving his God. Of course, I know that is not so, but at that time I had not been made aware of the difficulties confronting him that, since, have been lifted from his shoulders. Thus the momentary impression his words made upon me.

Yet I felt there was so much still to contribute. True, the parish is running smoothly. Equally true, it has reached a plateau in the respect and admiration of the townspeople where it has gone far beyond mere tolerance and acceptance.

To the ordinary ordained clergyman it would be sufficient to rest on one's laurels. Robert, however, is far from ordinary. That night when we were discussing the matter, I told him that now that everything was going smoothly, now that he had built up the church to the point where it is relatively impossible to build it further, he should expand the church's interest to an adjunct. And this is where I believe your excellent idea can bear fruit. In connection with the church Robert should encourage the construction of a rehabilitation school or center for juveniles who have become delinquent in their social behavior. The need for this is very great, and I believe the vestry and Robert would do well to consider it.

One does not stop because he has completed one job. He keeps building on it, adding here and there until he has recreated the structure, making it more beautiful and more superior. No man's work is ever done—not really. And that is why I believe Robert's future still lies ahead of him. It is a future that offers so much in contributory effort. Those of us who have tried to serve others are often tempted to serve ourselves, and when we do we regret it. Dear God! Don't I know how much! One cannot serve God and man, but often by serving God one generally finds one is serving man too.

July 19, 1953

My dear friend:

First of all permit me to offer you my condolences on the death of your brother. I know that no words of mine can possibly fill the void left in your spirit by so great a tragedy; yet, it is to be remembered, I believe, that the transition from a carnal to a spiritual state does not invariably preclude the existence of the one who has passed through that transition.

I like to believe (and I feel it is a true belief) that death is merely the means by which an individual passes from the carnal to the spiritual state of life; that life still goes on; and that man, in making his transition to his spiritual state, remains with us, although we are unable to perceive him with our carnal senses.

I believe that man, after death, has it within his power to advance himself along a far higher and superior plane of life than he had ever known during his pre-death experience. I do not feel that anyone who has made this transition is ever really apart from those who have not yet done so. You and I and the rest of mankind, chained, as we are, to time and eternity, can feel less of a loss, I think, than that which we would have ourselves believe exists. In a way, to feel otherwise would be to deny the omnipotence of God and the promise of eternal life.

In the days of my travels across Europe, before war cast its blight upon the continent and Communist incursions despoiled the Balkan nations of their freedom, I was in close touch and communication with a gentleman who was a representative of the University of Belgrade in Yugoslavia. He was of middle age then. Just prior to the commencement of the Second World War he entered the Greek Orthodox Church as a priest of that particular Christian faith. From that time on his life was a living hell, particularly as the country was torn apart by civil strife and, later, when the Communist hordes engulfed the nation and remained.

March 23, 1955

It was indeed a very great pleasure for me to receive your letter of February 9 along with the enclosed copy of a sermon you delivered to your congregation.

I read both with interest, and I have delayed in my reply to your letter because you asked me to comment on the sermon you sent. I wanted to read it several times so as to form a complete picture in my mind.

I realize you have presented your sermon to your people with the view in mind that you were speaking only of conditions as they exist in your immediate surroundings. Yet I cannot help but feel that what you said is true the world over. Mankind is in a bewildered state. Although you probably have brought the subject to the fore in other sermons, I think you failed to do so in this one. The subject being that Christianity is a religion based upon hope and faith. I feel that you have issued a warning to your people of dire things to come, rather than extending to them the message of hope and faith through love and charity with their neighbors, which is one of the reasons why Christ came to earth in human form.

I cannot help but believe that when God created the world and the vast cosmic universe wherein we dwell He created nothing that was displeasing in His sight, and when He created man He found man good to look upon. He gave man free will, and it is some of the things man has done by means of his free will that has made God frown and, in a sense, cause Him to send His son to earth to teach us the Christian morality whereby He wishes man to live. To a very large degree, as you have pointed out, we have not yet fulfilled His expectations.

Christian morality is the foundation and the basis for our existence in a Christian world, and whether we like it or not, we must adhere to the concepts of morality upon which our Christian religion is based. If we do not do so, sooner or later we will be given cause to regret it.

I have stated that it is my belief God created nothing displeasing in His sight. That includes man. I believe that if, in nothing else, each one of us is equal in the sight of God, God bestows His intense love and affection on us equally. But He has also seen fit to bless us with the gift of free will. Therefore, we have the right to make our own mistakes. We are able to think, and learning from past mistakes, we should be able to guide our steps accordingly. But man has not done this, and since he has refused to learn from his mistakes, such refusal has redounded to his detriment.

There is no escaping the fact that if an individual transgresses moral law, sooner or later he will receive a just punishment either in this world or the next. If his moral and ethical standards are of a very high calibre it is quite possible that his punishment will result in his being hounded and pursued by an unrelenting conscience until such time as he satisfies his outraged morality by making restitution to that moral law or code of ethics he has transgressed. If his standards of Christian morality and ethics are of a very low calibre, then the chances are that he will not be bothered by the rumblings of conscience while living in this world. But, as I said, punishment must come sooner or later.

As I believe that God loves and cherishes mankind individually and collectively I cannot believe He would want to destroy that which He loves. Therefore, I feel that if man does not possess a full Christian concept of ethical morality and practice in this life, he must learn it and practice it in the next life before he is worthy to face his Creator and abide with Him. Here on this earth we are given an opportunity to learn and practice this. If we fail in this life, I believe that in the next life we must practice through penance that which we failed to practice here. I believe that the soul of man is immortal. Therefore, when penance is complete we will stand face to face with our Creator and abide with Him throughout all eternity.

As you are probably aware, within the past fifty-five years a different concept of morality has arisen: one that, in practice, is not based upon the simple Christian ethic of love thy neighbor as thyself. The philosophy upon which this new morality is based has grown so greatly throughout the world that, in many cases, it has caused the moral bewilderment whereof you speak. In my opinion today's concept of morality is anti-Christian.

October 14, 1956

Thank you very much for your photograph and for the copy of the note addressed by President Harding to Dr. Pupin that you enclosed with your letter. Please let me also extend to you my heartiest felicitations on the occasion of your seventieth birthday. Indeed, you have reached a golden age with a wealth of years and experience behind you and the prospect of still more constructive endeavor ahead of you.

I was much interested in reading your statement "It is true we must always realize the life as it is. We priests, particularly in the villages, are in the position to observe man's nullity when we perform the burial. . . ."

With this statement I do not believe I can agree even in part. I cannot believe that man is ever a nullity, even in death. He is a creation of Divine Intent endowed with the awesome gift of free will. Therefore, his life, both before death and after it, is anything but a nullity. Since man was divinely created, there is, I feel, within each man a spark of divinity which, no matter what his circumstances, can never be destroyed. His reason occasionally forces him to fear death, but this fear, I think, may arise from a sense of guilt rather than from a sense of the unknown. And when man passes from the earthly picture it is possible that we, observing the lifeless body, might regard this as being a nullity. But to do so it is necessary to disregard man himself who inhabited the body. This, however, we cannot do because to lose sight of the spiritual entity that actually is man and to regard him as being a material being dependent upon material sustenance for survival (and that type of being only) is to lose sight of the spiritual creation God intended man to be.

I was very much interested to read what you had to say concerning the cultural life of your village, but I was much more interested and much more impressed with what you did not say. Of course, I realize there is very little that can be done to raise immediately the living standards of the people whom you describe, but by rendering unto God the things that are God's you might, by dedicating yourself to it, assist in raising their cultural standards. In my opinion a priest must live not for himself but for his people.

May 24, 1957

I am a great deal younger than you are, and possibly I think a bit differently from the way you do, but I feel it is unfortunate that you find it necessary to retire from work. Everyone should work, whether he is wealthy or poor; it gives a man dignity and adds to the meaning of life. I hope that I will never have to retire. Probably I may have to someday; still, it is important, I think, that everyone should keep busy.

If you are no longer going to be an active clergyman, then you should think of some way to fill your time—I mean, the time you have left.

Right now you are probably thinking how wonderful it will be to just sit in the sun and lead a slow and peaceful existence. I do not believe that such a thing exists. Man was brought into this world to struggle and to learn, and old age is no less a struggle than is youth. I believe that in order for man to retain his dignity he must always continue to work at something. It is true that a man of your age can hardly be expected to work in a garden with a pick or a shovel, but I think that, now, your contribution to mankind should be in the realm of the promulgation of ideas. You should contribute to your fellow man what you have learned over the years, and in this way you continue to justify your existence. No man is an island unto himself. He must always live with his fellow man. No matter how much we may wish it, we do not have the right for peace and solitude when our fellow man hungers and thirsts after a knowledge we may possess. It is my opinion that our lives are not given to us that we should live them for ourselves, but that we must live them for others. In this I don't think God gave us any choice, and I am sure that you, as a clergyman, can do nothing but agree.

I know that in your country it is a little different from mine, where a difference of opinion is not so quickly resented, but when I say you should keep yourself busy it is for your own peace of mind that I mention it.

November 1, 1958

Your letter of October 24th arrived after I had addressed and mailed another note to you. I have read this letter several times because it was of unusual interest.

What interested me most in your letter, as in others, was not what you said, but what you didn't say, and it is about this I would like to speak to you.

Before I begin, however, I probably should tell you that I have searched my own mind in order to ascertain whether or not I have the right to tell you what it is I wish to say. For the past two days I have been here at my house saying to myself that it is easy enough for me to sit here in the comfortable security of my home and tell someone else what he ought to do; that I don't have to undergo what he is undergoing; and that I couldn't have the remotest conception of the physical, mental, and spiritual privations you are being forced to sustain. But, after receiving your letter of October 24th I do feel I should tell you what is on my mind even though you may regard it as an impertinence, coming from someone who is young enough to be your son.

You have mentioned the spirit of anti-Christianity that seems to pervade your village and the low ebb of spiritual morality that, apparently, pervades the young. You have also spoken of your own modest circumstances in your temporal way of life.

I am in full agreement that some way must be found for you to survive physically, and not just survive but to live modestly and comfortably. This, I feel, is necessary for you. I also feel that you are acting correctly in endeavoring to start classes in English and in translating papers for the copper company. This will be of service to you in keeping your body alive.

But as a priest, you have a duty to your parish. I know you have only recently moved to Majdanpek, and it may be that you are not too well known there. But have you ever stopped to think why you were sent to Majdanpek in the first place? If God had a hand in sending you there, certainly He must have had His reasons. If the villagers are as bad off, spiritually, as you paint them, that is probably why you are there. It is obvious you will make no progress with them through church services. Therefore, the only way you are going to be able to enhance their spiritual and moral well-being is by the example of your own morality and by the strength of your personality. You will fail in many cases, and in this you will not be alone. Everything that Christ did, for example, was a complete failure until Calvary.

And yet even through the glossy sheen of immorality that you see in the youth of your village there must be something good and fine. For certainly no man can be all bad. There must be some good in him somewhere. It is a challenge for you to find it and to bring it out. I don't think any man really wants to live a life of immorality. I think every man is searching for the destiny of his soul, looking for something to which he can cling and in which he can believe. After you obtain their confidence this is something you might be able to provide, and it is probably for this reason God intended that you should go to Majdanpek. You cannot be blunt or brutal, but must act with tact, forbearance, and, above all, discretion. You see, sir, there is very little difference between the times in which we live and the period of the Roman Empire. Only the names are changed; that is all.

Part II

THE SOCIAL ORDER

When I was a small boy a young woman, who was destined to have an influence for good upon the lives of all of us, came to the back door of our home. My mother had employed her to work with the other members of the household staff, and she was with us for more than a quarter of a century. Eventually, as the years took their toll, she became infirm, and she retired to the home of her nephew. I have never forgotten her. I don't see how I ever could.

February 16, 1978

Word has just reached me that on Monday next you will be celebrating your ninetieth birthday. That is quite a milestone, and I did so want to write to you, particularly on this special occasion.

I go back to Pottsville about twice a year, and when I do I stay in the old house at Fifteenth Street and Mahantongo. Everything is gone now. All of the furnishings have either been distributed among us or have been sold. In the silence I often wander from room to room. The house stands there empty.

We can never go back to that which was in the days when the house was vibrant and alive and we all congregated on the side porch for cocktails before Sunday dinner; we can now only observe those times with a backward glance. Perhaps it is just as well. All of us change with time, and what was suitable for us half a century ago is not always that which is suitable for us now. We are a different people from those who lived in that house those many years so long ago, different but still the same. Time has a tendency for change and, with time, so have we.

Dad and Mother and Dohrman are gone now. Augusta and Frederick and Dick and I have all proceeded along our separate ways. This is as it should be.

I hope this letter finds you well. You helped raise me, and I know I can never forget the many services you rendered to me and to all of us when you were with us and when we were all together.

June 7, 1968

My dear friend:

I read your letter with much interest, and I am in complete sympathy with what you have said concerning the problems of your nephew and his parents. For every action there is a re-action—an effect for every cause—and we should have seen it coming and expected what has happened, but very few of us did.

The attitude of the youth of today has its background and beginnings somewhere in the maelstrom of the social experimentation that commenced with the Roosevelt Administration some thirty-five years ago. During that period the seeds were planted that were to germinate and grow into what is today's moral laxity and sociological indifference. This was the time that social welfare, sponsored and financially supported by taxpayers' funds, had their beginning.

It did not happen all at once. It began with a small program here and another one there, and then another one was added and something else was added after that, with the federal government assuming more and more of the guardianship over the enterprise of the American people. This continued to snowball until, finally, what had been a self-reliant people began to depend more and more upon their federal, state, and local governments to do for them what they had been accustomed to doing for themselves.

Whether government subsidies are right or wrong is not the point. It is what has happened to the American people as a result of government paternalism that is important. Partly, as a result of this there has taken place an erosion of self-reliance. This has occurred over the many years. In September of 1939, when Europe embarked on the Second World War, this erosion was still in the making and had progressed minimally. That is why, two years and a few months later, when the disaster of Pearl Harbor struck the American people in stunned and shocked surprise, the entire nation was able to band together and fight with grim willingness, determination, and sacrifice.

Four years later, when the war was over, the boys who had been overseas returned and fathered a generation, and this generation has now grown up. Not all of them, but a large number of them, have grown up in an aura of permissiveness which had its commencement at the beginning of the Second World War. It was during this era that jobs were both plentiful and lucrative in the factories and plants engaged in the manufacture of war matériel throughout the nation. And with the vast armies of the male population of our country engaged on the battlefields of the world it was many a mother or wife and in some cases many a teen-aged son who neglected their duties as housewife and/or high-school student in order to seize an opportunity to augment family or personal income. In itself, this was fine, but in a large number of cases, along with the added income, it produced parental neglect; and children, having a tendency to grow up, did so, in some cases subject to their own whims and wishes.

They went through elementary school, secondary school, and college, and in not a few cases they were taught by teachers whose yearly salaries amounted to three thousand dollars a year, if that. Many of these teachers were really dedicated men and women, but they were also human; and being aware of their social and financial frustration on the one hand and noting on the other the social and economic security of the entrepreneur, the educator tended to express his resentment by an adherence to intellectual and social philosophies that had as their purpose a redistribution of the wealth of the nation. The educator found himself, in many cases, teaching what was a complete negation of the principles of American life. While this is not true of all, it certainly was true of some. Added to this was the infiltration into the American educational system by members of the international Communist movement, and the climax of all of this was reached by a Supreme Court decision that forbade the dismissal of a teacher solely on the basis of that teacher's being a member of the Communist Party.

There were other factors contributing to the growth of the new generation. There was the principle of progressive education, which had as its compelling force the theory that a child should decide for himself when to study and what to study, and that the disciplining of a child should be made a thing of the past. There also existed in the home and in the school a moral vacuum because of the de-emphasis of religion in both institutions.

Finally, there were economic considerations. Prices were going up. One thing that had a direct bearing upon the members of the New Generation was their personal appearance. Haircuts used to be fifty cents; then they went up to a dollar and a dollar and a half. In many places to two dollars, two and a half and three. Again, the reason for the price rise is not the issue. But to a man of moderate means or less, who had three or four children to raise and support, this was a very big bite out of the family's income every three or four weeks. So he either cut the children's hair himself, and he usually did a very poor job of it, or he permitted their hair to grow long. Eventually, long hair among the young became a mark of distinction, and that and sloppy attire were eventually adopted by the younger generation as badges of rebellion against parental restraint. All of these were and are factors in the growth and development of our progeny, your nephew included.

And what can we do about it? How can we correct our mistakes? We live with it, for there is nothing else we can do. And we pray and we hope that when our sons and daughters rear their own families, as they are beginning to do now, they will realize how they themselves were brought up and will instill in their children the religious and moral principles inherent in man.

Somewhere near the western and midsection of the Canadian border a rather distraught woman lived with her stepson. She had been brought up in the principles and beliefs of an older generation and adhered to them religiously. A moral confrontation existed between her and her stepson, and it was for this reason that this letter was written.

July 21, 1966

Your letter gave me somewhat of a shock, for I had not known of the embarrassment and humiliation you are enduring. I have met your stepson, and to all intents and purposes I found him to be a fine young man. It is most evident that while each of you cares for the other most deeply, he does not realize what you are going through. It is quite possible he regards what he is doing as socially acceptable behavior according to the "new morality" of his generation. However, we both know that even up there on the Canadian border where you live there are standards of social behavior that are the same which you and I have known and to which we have adhered as did past generations.

One does not bring one's mistress into his home and flaunt her in front of his mother. Certainly he would never be permitted to do a thing like that if his father were still alive. He wouldn't dare. I knew Edward very well, and I know he wouldn't have stood still a minute for this.

And I can understand your point of view, too, and why you can't put your foot down. You are afraid he will leave home and you will be there alone. It is a very subtle form of blackmail, but I don't think your stepson realizes that this is what he is doing. The last time I was up your way I had occasion to talk with him, but not on this particular subject. He was very pleasant, and we spoke mostly about you. It was easy, through this conversation, to see how much he loves and admires you and regards you as his true mother rather than as his stepmother. I am sure he doesn't have the remotest idea you feel the way you do.

And what should you do? For the time being endure it until such time as an opportunity will present itself whereby he will come to a realization of what he is doing to you. Then he will have to choose, and it must be of his own volition, as a result of his examination of his own conscience. You must in no way influence his decision. And if he decides the way I think he will decide, he will keep his mistress but will no longer bring her to your home. This would, indeed, be a fair compromise.

August 6, 1975

My dear friend:

Your letter was most interesting, particularly that part of it appertaining to your college acquaintance who appears to be getting himself into deep water. He is alone and lonely and, probably, will be for the rest of his life. He has tried drugs; they are a failure. He has tried suicide and that too has failed, whether because he unintentionally blundered the attempt or intentionally blundered it because he didn't really intend for it to be successful to begin with.

You cannot help him, my friend. As matters stand now, he will be condemned by society for the rest of his days, and if he remains as he is, he will have very little happiness in this world in this society. He is here on earth for a purpose, and in line with that purpose (you and I, and probably he, have no idea what it is) he can do one thing. He can do as Michelangelo did when faced with the same sexual confrontation. He can accept himself as he is, and he can create beauty and intelligence in the field of endeavor in which he is most competent. But more than anything else, he has to possess the will and the determination to survive, to live with himself as he is, or to change himself if he feels that he can and that it is necessary. And he can only do this by himself. The only thing you can do for him is to point it out to him, but you cannot do it for him. He must look at his life, make up his own mind; and the decision has got to be his.

If he does succeed in his suicide attempts the world will have lost a creative being (for each of us is creative in his own small way), and the world will be that much poorer because he is no longer with us. But the greater loss will be his because he will go to his God with his earthly mission unaccomplished.

Perhaps it is intended he should be a pederast. Possibly this may be the only way he can learn the lessons he is to be taught while here and also gain the will and determination that possibly will be required of him both here and elsewhere. As I have said: All of this is something he will have to face, himself. Let us hope he does.

November 25, 1969

Dear Steve:

At this moment things are relatively quiet, and for that I am grateful. The Optimist Club Youth Appreciation Banquet was held last Thursday. I had intended to go but didn't, and therein lies a tale.

The preceding Thursday we were at the Golden Gloves Boxing Tournament when it was decided that certain members and their wives would meet at the home of one of us for cocktails before we went to the banquet. Guess at whose house the cocktails were served! The vote was unanimous minus one. The answer to my unasked question was that everyone else lived farther out, and that my house was closer to the Ramada Inn, where the banquet was being held. That wasn't the reason; that was the answer. The others also arranged who were to be invited. I was told my job was to supply the house, the liquor, and the hors d'oeuvres.

I had some oysters (raw) as part of the hors d'oeuvres, but I had no way of opening them. I went out and bought an oyster knife and a pair of gloves. One needs only one glove so that in the event the knife slips one doesn't cut one's hand. I had a little trouble with the gloves. I went to the Five and Ten and bought a pair of work gloves. They cost a dollar. I told the girl at the counter what they were for and asked if I could buy just one glove for half price. She looked at me for a moment (and it was a very long moment) and said: "Look, Sport! Why don't you buy both of them and use the one you want? You can give the other one to the Goodwill Industries and take it off your income tax." For want of anything more to say I had to pay the dollar.

We had a fine time at the cocktail party. The only difficulty was that only one couple went to the banquet, although all of us had tickets. I have been trying to get a refund on my ticket ever since, but I was told that it was my own fault I wasn't there and that there would be no refunds given out. The next day was our regular meeting of the Optimist Club, and since I was the one who gave the party, I was fined a dollar because the president said I was the instigator in keeping the others from going to the banquet.

I don't know whether you know what the remains of a last night's party look like the following morning. I do.

Fortunately, all of the wives dragged their husbands home, so I didn't have that to contend with. I got up at eleven and remembered I had just an hour to get dressed and get down to the Optimist Club luncheon. Actually, it was the last thing in the world I wanted to do. My mouth felt as if the Russian Army had walked through it. I brushed my teeth, gargled with Listerine, and took a couple of aspirin. Then I went downstairs and took one appalled look at the ghastly mess I discovered in the living room. I was ready to turn around and go right back to bed again. But I shaved and dressed and came downstairs again, keeping my eyes averted from the living room because I was hoping that maybe, just maybe, if I didn't look at it it would go away. It didn't. I went through the kitchen on my way to the garage, and there was just as much of a mess there. Then, after the luncheon was over, I drove out to Trans-Matic (our vocational training school) and got one of the students to come in ($1.50 an hour) and clean up the mess. As I write this everything is back to normal, or, at least, as back to normal as it can be—which isn't saying much.

Individuals, I suppose, during the course of time, tend to divide themselves into two groups: Those who, for whatever rhyme or reason, conduct a war against society and those who do not. I presume that these two catagories can be subdivided still further. At certain times and for certain reasons we become acquainted with individuals from each of these catagories, and those of us who are not at war with society can look at those who are and say: "There but for the Grace of God go I." In that context the following letter was written.

August 28, 1975

Your two letters are on my desk waiting to be answered. I am, at the moment, trying to reply to your inquiry concerning boxing managers. Probably the only people who could give you the information you wish would be the National Boxing Association of America. I have called the public library to find out if they could get the address for me, and I am waiting for them to call me back now. I think that if you write to the association they can give you much more information than I can. Mention, particularly, the area of the country in which you expect to be living. Since you have people in Montana who have agreed to be responsible for you, that is probably the only area in the country to which you will be paroled. I don't know, of course. This is just a guess. If I were you I would see what managers are available up there.

But, son, you really do have to have a definite plan or idea of what you are going to do when you are paroled, and if I were you I would get cracking on it. If I were on that parole board and you were to come up before me for consideration of parole, I would want to see a completely realistic plan of what you intend to do when you are released, letters from people in Montana guaranteeing that you will be employed, and letters from people guaranteeing you a place to live. That is, assuming you have little or no resources to take care of your financial obligation when you are released. More than that, I would also want to see an alternative plan in the event the first one did not work out.

I don't know what it is that you did to get where you are now, but I believe that unless you have a sensible, believable program for your future plus a sensible, believable backup program, and that you follow through on either one or the other after you are released, within a couple of months you will be right back where you are now or at some other penal institution. And I am sure you do not want that to happen. None of us does.

As you are aware, quite some time ago I owned a small apartment complex I called The Yuengling Arms. It was a headache from start to finish, and I am glad to be rid of it. Your ideas of how to run an apartment complex are fine but somewhat impractical for the one I owned. You wouldn't be able to rent to a higher clientele than I rented to because a higher clientele wouldn't be caught dead in that area of the city, and if they were, that's probably how they would be found.

Just to give you some idea of what you would be in for, let me tell you some of the unbelievable things that happened. I poured money into that place, and it was like pouring it down a rathole. The renters were in a low-income group, and, in this case, were completely irresponsible. They should have been living in the stalls of a barn rather than in houses. They would wantonly destroy something—anything—as the whim took them, mainly because it didn't belong to them and they didn't feel any responsibility for it.

At one time we had a group of Indian boys who were students at a vocational training school. These boys were sent to the school for rehabilitation training to become automobile mechanics, and they lived in my apartments. Every Saturday they would turn in to the manager their zip guns, knives, clubs, blackjacks, etc., because they knew they were going out and get drunk that night, and they knew they were going to get into a fight, and they didn't want to kill each other. This happened every Saturday night, and it generally continued until Monday. The police were there constantly. For that matter, so was the Board of Health.

Finally, after we got rid of the students (and that name is certainly a misnomer), the fighting died down, and a more mature but equally impecunious clientele moved in. During the period of my naivete I would get calls from the Salvation Army or the Welfare Department asking me if I had accommodations, and I usually did. They would offer to pay the first month's rent for someone they wanted to send over, and there would be a hint that there was a job opportunity for the individual soon to come. Somehow or other that job opportunity never did materialize, and after the first month I was stuck with someone who couldn't pay his rent, and it was a difficult job getting him out.

Eventually my manager left, and I got another one. He was a young man in his very early twenties, married, and from the Bible-belt area of the country. He wasn't overly bright, but then, one had to take what one could get. He and his wife moved into the manager's cottage, and his mother moved in with them. I hadn't counted on the mother, but then, there were a lot of other things I hadn't counted on, either. The three of them were like most of my tenants. They didn't have a dime among them. The mother was a staunch, Bible-thumping revivalist who, when the preacher would give a hell-fire and damnation sermon, would be the first to shout: Hallelujah!

I remember a couple with three children who moved into Cottage Three. Their name, oddly enough, was Felicity, and he worked nights at a printing establishment. Across the way from Cottage Three was Cottage Ten, where a young Indian boy lived, aged approximately twenty-two, regular and pleasant features, and a muscular body. At least, that is how it appeared to Mrs. Felicity because Mr. Felicity worked nights, and after he had gone to work Mrs. Felicity would pay a neighborly call on the young Indian boy to listen to him strum his guitar. Who was staying with the children I have no idea. Finally, the guitar playing would stop, the lights would go out, and everyone would know that the young Indian boy was giving Mrs. Felicity a little felicity of his own.

Nobody cared, either, except one person—the manager's mother. She saw sin rampant and exultant over there in Cottage Ten, and she swooped down like an avenging angel. Girded with the Sword of Righteousness and armed in the full knowledge of her duty, she told Mr. Felicity everything that had been going on and a lot more that hadn't. Mr. Felicity went after the Indian boy with a gun. The Indian boy cleared out of there in a hurry, and nobody ever saw him again. Mr. Felicity packed up his family and moved to a different location, and I lost two roomers and their rent money. To the manager's mother that was inconsequential. She was righteousness personified. She had renounced the devil and all his works, the pomp and vanity of this wicked world, and all the sinful lusts of the flesh. She had cleansed the temple of Sin and Corruption and now stood there, triumphant at Armageddon. Hallelujah!

After that the manager's mother didn't last long. Eventually, she moved somewhere else, and things settled down to normal; at least, as normal as it was possible for them to be.

There was a young girl who resided there. She had gone into business for herself, and she used her cottage as her business establishment. Needless to say, business prospered, and she was the only one who ever paid her rent promptly and on time. Her clientele was always most interesting. Unfortunately, she didn't stay very long. She was an ambitious young woman, and she was anxious to get to the top in her profession. She accepted a free-rent offer from one of her clients and moved out. I was, indeed, sorry to see her go—financially speaking, that is.

January 15, 1967

Dear Curtis:

As you are aware I have been in Pottsville over the Christmas holidays. I returned on the sixth. While on my way back to Phoenix I stopped in Oklahoma City to spend the night. I was rather tired and went to bed around ten o'clock. While I was brushing my teeth I heard someone running down the corridor outside my room, and a girl calling for help. Then I heard a heavier tread running after her, a door slam, and a pounding on a door down the hall. I opened my door and looked into the corridor, and here was a young man walking up without a stitch of clothing on, naked as the day he was born, and muttering something that sounded like "Dumb broad!" He saw me, nodded, and walked on.

I didn't tell this story to my Ward because I thought he would think I had been staying at a cheap hotel. The room cost five dollars a night. I did, however, tell it to an Optimist

Club luncheon meeting, and one of the members said: "Well, you did stay at a crummy hotel!" Another one looked up from his plate and said: "I know where you were staying, and it wasn't at a hotel."

Everything seems to happen to me.

Divorce and/or separation between married people can be a source of tragedy and desolation not only for the couple, themselves, but for their families and friends and all those who love them. It sometimes becomes so trying that you want to knock their heads together to get them to see things in a rational manner, but if you ever decide you want to try that method, don't! It doesn't work. This letter was addressed to a lovely woman who was married to a fine man.

February 25, 1975

By this time you should have had ample opportunity to think over your decision in favor of a separation from Charles. I believe you are aware I have long been opposed to separation and/or divorce in any case, unless, of course, one of the parties is acting toward the other in a completely unreasonable manner or in an irrational attitude. But then, I have never been married to Charles (although when we all lived at the fraternity house there were a number of us who thought Charles could be a bit heavy), and looking at it from Charles' point of view, I've never been married to you either. So, maybe you're both to blame.

I am sure you must realize what the breaking up of a home can mean to your children, even though the majority of them are now fully grown and on their own. They may feel it necessary to take sides and, if they do, that invariably hurts the other parent or, in many cases, both. It is the rending of the protective fabric of the home and all that the home represents in love, stability, and security for them, and it is not uncommon for them to experience a feeling of loss and bewilderment.

I am, of course, an outsider in your and Charles' private affairs, and that is as it should be. But I know you have had more than thirty years of married life. All of it couldn't have been sheer hell. There must have been something in there that gave you both reason to love one another and to live together in marriage for so long a period of time.

If I were you, I would go back over that life to the happy and productive times, reviewing them and noting why they were happy and productive for you. Then go back to the tragic times and contemplate and discover why they were tragic times for you. Then go back over the years you feel were happy and productive years for Charles (they may or may not be the same years as yours) and those that were tragic for him. Analyze them and compare the reasons for Charles' with the reasons for your own. You may be surprised at the conclusions you reach. If Charles ever asked me I would give him the same advice. You didn't ask me, either, but you got it anyway.

Charles can be as stubborn and as pigheaded as an old mule. All of us knew this who lived at the fraternity house with him when we were in college. We all respected and honored him too. And while I mention that about Charles, you must remember, at the same time, you're not too easy to live with either. Both of you have my love.

December 26, 1977

Dear Jim:

Christmas is at an end, and for that I am grateful. I mean, of course, the hustle and bustle of the holiday which, I guess, I enjoyed much more when I was younger. I don't enjoy downing scotch after scotch and making small talk, and that's what these past couple of days have been. I guess you might say I am in a "Bah! Humbug" mood. The older I get the more I sympathize with Scrooge.

Tomorrow I am giving a dinner party for fourteen. If I were doing this in my own home I would go out of my mind, but I am in Pottsville, Pennsylvania, right now, and the hotel is doing it. That is one relief. The other one is that on Wednesday I go down to Alexandria and visit with Captain and Mrs. Raish and then, the following day, I take the plane back to Phoenix. There I can relax in my own home.

I flew to Pennsylvania this season instead of motoring. I had planned to motor, but I also bought a plane ticket in case the weather should change my plans. It did. The day I was to leave Phoenix by car a violent storm began to form in upper Minnesota or lower Canada, and it was sweeping to the southeast. It arrived in Illinois just about the same time I would have if I had been motoring, so I thought it would be best to go by plane.

I went via American Airlines nonstop to Philadelphia and then on a dinky little airline called Altair out of Philadelphia to Harrisburg, by prop plane no less. I haven't been on one of those things since I traveled on the Rhodesian Airlines from Victoria Falls to Johannesburg. That was an experience too. The plane (Philadelphia) was late boarding, and it was late getting off the ground because there were so many other planes taking off ahead of us, and there were, of course, others that were landing. Then the stewardess turned out the lights in the plane, and we sat there, not quite in total darkness, stewing. We couldn't read to pass the time while we waited. Maybe there was a reason for this idiocy for turning out the lights, but for the life of me I can't imagine what it would be.

I do not know where you are. I would presume, by this time, you are about to leave for or are in Okinawa. I would suppose it to be an excellent place in which to pass the winter (weatherwise, that is), but that is all. Other than that I don't envy you in the slightest.

Your becoming a father again is most interesting. I am delighted to hear it. This time I hope it will be a boy. Then you can have a junior. I hope Louise is well, and I hope you don't have to leave for Okinawa before the child is born. That, surely, would be unfortunate.

July 11, 1977

Dear Jim:

Thank you for your letter expressing an interest in obtaining a good investment policy. I am most interested in that subject too, and I have followed certain rules which I believe to be of value.

I do not profess to be a financial counselor, and what I do I do only for the purpose of establishing an income and continuing to build upon it and increase its growth. So far, I have found it to be quite successful. It can be of use to a small investor or a large investor, depending upon the size of your investment.

I would suggest to you, first of all, that you decide how much money you can afford to put aside weekly or monthly. When you have made this decision, do it. Even if there is one particular week or month you feel you don't want to or can't afford to, do it anyway, because if you don't do it one week you may feel less inclined to do so the following week and/or some of the weeks thereafter.

When you have decided upon the amount of money you wish to set aside each week and/or month, put this amount of money in a special bank account opened just for this purpose, regularly every week or month. When you go to bed at night take the change out of your pocket and add this to that sum of money.

When that particular bank account has reached the sum of three or four or five hundred dollars, withdraw it from your account, leaving sufficient funds in the account so that it will remain active. Go to a stockbroker so you can arrange for the purchase of at least ten shares (more, if possible) of a first-class stock selling at a reasonable price and offering a good dividend.

You should investigate these stocks yourself. Your broker, if he is reputable and reliable, will have all the information concerning the background of the company whose stock you choose to purchase. Among other things, you should look and see how long it has been paying dividends, whether there have been years or a year in which it didn't pay a dividend, and why it didn't. You should look to see what its debt is and whether or not the debt is too extensive for the business the company is doing. Check the company's rating. Is the stock regarded as an A-1 stock or is it regarded less favorably? Check its safety factor and determine whether or not it is a purely speculative stock or a relatively safe one for investment purposes. These are just a few of the things to look for. There are others.

When you have made up your mind, purchase the stock and

then start all over again; but this time, when the dividend arrives, don't touch it. Put that in the bank account too. When your bank account has reached the required amount, draw out the money, but this time purchase a different stock. In that way, and if you continue this procedure faithfully, you will eventually have an excellent, diversified portfolio, and if you start it now, by the time you are in your forties you will have a very nice income coming in.

You will make mistakes; that is true. You will win a few and you will lose a few, but if you are not a dolt—and I'm sure you're not—you will learn from your mistakes, and gradually you will increase your knowledge and experience to the point where you will make fewer and fewer mistakes and become more sure of yourself. This is true in anything.

This, my friend, is, I think, all I can tell you. These are the basics. The rest of it is up to you and to your desire to increase your income. If you have any questions, please keep in touch with me. Another point: knowing when and what to sell is just as important as knowing when and what to buy.

Approximately ten years ago, maybe longer, while traveling through Canada I made the acquaintance of a young Scotsman who had only recently emigrated to that country. We became very good friends, and I have been in constant communication with him and his family ever since. He made one error that he will probably never make again. Thinking that he could do better financially at or near the site of the new oil discovery in the North Sea, he and his family returned to Scotland. The correspondence in the several letters that follow relate to his experiences.

September 29, 1976

Why do you persist? You returned to Scotland in order to secure better and more remunerative employment than you had in Winnipeg. You purchased a rather rundown house, and you secured employment. You found that it was not as remunerative as you had hoped, and you began making repairs on your house so you could sell it and return to Canada. You then discovered that the person you hired to repair your house was costing you as much as you were making, so you quit your job and began doing the work yourself. That meant you had no income coming in, and you had to live off your savings: you, your wife, and your three children.

You should realize that every day you stay in Scotland is going to cost you more money and, as a Scotsman, you should know about things like that.

Between the end of May, when I spoke with you on the telephone while I was in London, until now you have had ample time to put your house in sufficient order so that you would be able to sell it. Place the damn thing in the hands of a broker now! Let him sell it for you, and don't wait around until he does. Get back to Canada immediately. Get all your stuff packed (the boys too) and get back there for your own sake so that you can start earning a living for yourself and for your family.

An article in the *National Geographic Magazine* says that Edmonton, Fort McMurray, and the area around there and to the north in Alberta are booming with newly discovered oil. Prospectors are flocking up there and to Yellowknife. There is a proposed gas pipeline to be run from Inuvki, near the northern border of the Yukon Territory, south to Edmonton. The people who are running this oil consortium in Edmonton and to the north are Panarctic Oils Limited. If you prefer something like that, get in touch with them. I do not know their address, but you can find that out by going to the commercial attaché of the Canadian consulate in whatever large city is near you where a Canadian consulate is located: Edinburgh, I should think.

If you would prefer to stay in Winnipeg, write a letter to your former employers and tell them you are returning and would like to work for them. They will probably welcome you with open arms. But whatever you do, get moving now.

November 17, 1976

You are probably correct in that the only way you are going to retain the value of your funds is by purchasing something of value in the United Kingdom and selling it for equal or more value in Canada. Antiques are always good. I would not buy a car, because you would have a heavy duty to pay in Canada if you did. Antiques, books, things like that do not have duties placed upon them, at least, here in the United States. Paintings also are included in this list. You will have to have a contact, a dealer, in Canada who will be willing to purchase the article from you outright or will be willing to accept it and try to sell it for you on consignment. I would suggest Montreal or Ottawa, possibly Toronto.

I would suggest a painting from a reputable dealer in London or Edinburgh, possibly Southby's in London. Get a painting by a well-known artist, either alive or dead: a Goya, a Tintoretto, a Picasso, a Van Gogh, there are any number of them; but get one by an artist (preferably dead) who sells well, and get it authenticated by the dealer from whom you purchase it. Tell him why you are doing this and what you are planning to do, and he probably can help you by giving you a letter of introduction to his contacts in Canada. This, I think, is your best bet. Remember, though, your dealer in Scotland or England has to be reputable, and the most reputable house that I know in London is Southby's. I have never done business with them, but their reputation is world-wide.

September 17, 1977

I cannot tell you with what pleasure it was that I received your letter advising me of your return to Canada. I am afraid I have missed you this year. I was through Canada in late June and early July, and when I stopped at the Fort Garry Hotel in Winnipeg I sent you a card saying, in words to this effect, "It's your turn to have me to dinner. I am here. Where are you?" Now I see that next time I am going to have to reroute myself and, when near Lake Louise, take the highway north to Jaspar and go on to Edmonton, and then, the next day, south to Regina. I am looking forward to seeing Dorothy and the three boys.

It is good to know you are back. Apparently you sold the house in Ayershire, and I hope it was for a sum that was fair to you. I also hope you are not going to do anything as stupid as that again. I assume that by this time you have found a job you enjoy and can do well. Work at the job and, while doing so, teach the boys the skills you know so that they won't be starting out without some kind of an occupational background—that is, when they have completed their schooling and have entered the employment market.

When you get to know prospective customers or clients and they know you can and will do a good job, then you might go into business for yourself. Also, get to know the manager of your local bank so that he can get to know you and your reliability. You will find out soon enough when you're ready to start your own business. In the meantime, keep the money you have for that purpose in the bank or purchase certificates of deposit with it, anyway you can invest it with a good return and, at the same time, have it available to you when you will need it to start your business.

You and Dorothy and the boys should live off the income of your employment. That includes house payments if you can do all of that on your salary. It's going to be rough going for a while, as you probably have noticed. Don't dip into the principal amount of your savings unless you absolutely have to. You will need that for the time when you go into business for yourself, and when that time comes you may find out it is not you who owns the business. It is the business that owns you.

But I'm awfully glad you're back, my friend. Keep in touch with me. I am looking forward to seeing you and your family again. The boys must be approaching high-school age by now, aren't they?

Mothers are ambitious for their children. They have been ever since the time of Eve. They worry about everything, from the serious to the trivial. It is their nature to do so. One young mother was worried about her son's grammar and what it would mean to him in the future. I had an occasion to write the following letter to her.

March 17, 1965

I have your letter of a few days ago telling me of the difficulties in which you have been engaged concerning your son's seeming inability to master English grammar. I sympathize with both of you because I know I had the same difficulty myself when I was going to school, and I considered diagraming sentences a waste of time and utterly useless in learning to speak the English language correctly. I still do.

Believe me, my friend, when I tell you that your son is never going to learn correct grammatical usage in the classroom if he doesn't know it now. This is a subject he learns at home from you, because if the boy's parents do not use correct grammar in the home he is never going to use it in his everyday speech. His teacher can correct him until she is blue in the face, but it is not going to do any good, because the moment he is outside the classroom, he is going to revert to the kind of speech he hears at home and in the street: the kind to which he is accustomed. I have never known it to be any other way.

It is important that he use correct grammar in his everyday speech because the kind of work he does in the future may be determined by this. If he intends to be a professional man, such as an attorney or a doctor, or even become an actor or a minister, the ability to communicate and to communicate well is, to a considerable degree, his stock in trade. It will be important to him. It will also be important to him in his social activities with other people because if he does not use good grammar among people who do, he will be considered crass and will be looked down upon.

There is, however, something you can do, and this will benefit you as well as him.

Associate yourself with him in his learning. When he has been given scholastic assignments, share them with him. I don't mean you should do them for him, but assist him in the learning process by showing him how such problems or assignments should be completed. My mother once said she learned more by helping my brothers and me with our arithmetic than she ever learned when she was in school.

Eventually, there will come a time when he will surpass you in one or more of his subjects—possibly in all of them. Perhaps it might be in the field of arithmetic, perhaps in some other field. If this is so, then it would behoove you to study the problems in his textbook so that you can learn to do them yourself. I believe that in this way you can grow closer to your son, and you yourself will grow in wisdom and in knowledge.

To the vast majority of people children are a blessing. We love them despite the fact that as the years roll on, and they grow from boyhood to young manhood they say and do things that drive us absolutely out of our minds. The following comments were addressed to such a young man somewhere between the age of twelve and fifteen. He is older now, and were he to read these words again he just might take them seriously.

February 12, 1970

There are certain attributes and accomplishments one acquires or learns through the course of his years. Some are good and some are bad, but you must be able to ascertain which is which. In my opinion, and, I believe, in the opinion of many others, the most important personal attribute one can acquire is self-discipline.

The definition of self-discipline is difficult to put into words. For example, you are aware of the difference between right and wrong. Self-discipline can be regarded as the faculty of driving oneself to do what is right when it is much easier, and possibly more lucrative, to do what is wrong. It is, in a sense, the fulfilling of personal responsibility.

You must remember that for every privilege and right you possess there is a corresponding duty and responsibility you must fulfill. That is the way of life. If you purchase something, you must pay for it. If you steal something, you must in the end still pay for it in one way or another: possibly by imprisonment and the loss of your freedom, or in some other way, such as having to live with a guilty knowledge. But whatever it happens to be, rights and privileges go hand in hand with duties and responsibilities. Sometimes duty and responsibility entail an obligation to other people, such as your parents and your friends; but more often than not, they entail an obligation to yourself. That is why, when you go to school, you have an obligation to study.

There will come a time (and it will come frequently) when you will be faced with what appears to be a divergence of obligations. That is, when you are faced with an obligation to two different persons or ideals and when, if you accept the one, you will betray the other. Sometimes these are very difficult decisions to make, and it is then that you must base your decision on what you believe to be morally and legally right. Here your own self-discipline comes into play, because the chances are that there may be a great deal of pressure put upon you to make your decision opposite from what is actually should be. You must be strong enough to support what you believe to be morally and legally right.

Another thing you should have, my friend, is ambition. This never hurt anyone. You must set various goals for yourself, then try to achieve them.

Let me tell you of a very good friend of mine who has made quite a name for himself on the national political scene. Long before he was prominent we knew each other quite well, and he told me that at each stage of his life he made certain plans for his future. He set, as one of his goals, a time limit during which he would become a practicing attorney. During this stage in his career he finished school, went to college, and worked his way through college and Harvard Law School by waiting on tables and any other work he could get. When this was completed he set up another goal for himself, that of becoming a member of the Arizona State Legislature. Again he was successful. He worked hard to achieve the post and was an excellent representative.

His next goal was that of becoming governor of the State of

Arizona, and in this he was defeated. It was a bitter defeat because he had counted on it very much. But he had the self-discipline to accept defeat, put it behind him, reject the luxury of brooding about it and feeling sorry for himself, and he went ahead to something else. Today he is greatly admired and respected for his ability and integrity, and it wouldn't surprise me in the slightest to learn that when Senator Barry Goldwater or Senator Paul Fannin retire he would aspire to one of the seats held by Arizona in the United States Senate.

There is, however, one more point I think it would be wise for you to consider. Throughout your life you will be faced with many frustrations and disappointments, and some of them will be bitter indeed. Only you can develop the iron self-discipline necessary to cope with them. There will be many times when decisions will be made that will affect you personally, and that you will feel are absolutely and irretrievably wrong and unjust. In quite a number of cases they will be, and they will be most unfair too. The way you accept these decisions and what you personally do about them will determine the kind of man you are or are going to become.

Since the time when I first made their acquaintance I have retained an abiding respect for those who profess and practice the Amish faith. They are a hard-working and conscientious people, sincere in their beliefs and in their way of life. Many of their sons, at one time or another, have lived as honored guests in my home. There is always a welcome there for them whenever they choose to come.

July 14, 1976

Thank you so much for your letter. I can fully understand and appreciate your wish to have Charles remain in Lancaster with you, and were he my son, I would, beyond question, feel the same way. Charles telephoned me last Saturday to tell me he will be here on the evening of the eighteenth. Even if he would be returning to Lancaster immediately, he would still have to come here because his car, his guns, his clothing, and other items are all here.

The most I can do to honor your request is to advise you that I will not encourage Charles to stay, but at the same time, neither can I discourage him; and for two reasons. This is a decision Charles himself must make, and I do not feel I have any right to interfere with any decision he will make regarding where he will go and what he will do. The second reason is that for me to discourage him from staying here would result only in his going somewhere else, and more probably than not, it would not be back to Lancaster. I would also be violating my own tenets of hospitality were I to do so. Because I admire and respect the Amish people so much, I have made it a point that my home will always be open to those Amish boys who come here from Pennsylvania. I have found every one of them to be a fine, decent, God-fearing young man, honest and honorable beyond question. I would never open my home to any others.

Perhaps you and Charles' father would be interested in knowing how and why all of this came about.

Back in the days when the Vietnam War was in progress our friends John, Sam, and Alpheus and some of the other boys were completing their military service at various hospitals in this city. I met them here. They were working for mere pittances and had very little extra money. There were times when they were able to supplement their income by helping in the kitchen or in the dining room whenever my social obligations required me to give a dinner party. Quite frequently, too, I found it necessary to visit various other cities, states, and countries, and the boys stayed and lived at my house while I was gone. This insured the safety of the house from burglary, and at the same time it gave the boys a place to live where they wouldn't have to pay any rent.

After this had gone on for several years I thought to myself: Why not let them live here as long as they wish? There were three extra bedrooms and there was plenty of room. The boys would be free from having to pay rent, and if I were to be called away suddenly, such as in the case when my mother died, I could leave without worrying what was going to happen to the house.

When I went to Australia one year John Richard and another

young man were staying in the house, and when I returned there were two others there too. I had never met either of them until I walked into the house and saw a tall, nice-looking young man whom I had never seen before, sitting on the bed in one of the spare bedrooms, watching television. It was Charles. Pretty soon I heard the roar of a motorcycle and in came Elias. I had never seen or heard of him before either. But because the house was open to boys like John Richard and his friends, when Charles and Elias came out this way John Richard asked them to stay here and they did. That is how this whole thing started.

They do not stay without working. I believe they should have their own income to assist in supporting themselves. I do not believe a good day's work ever hurt anyone, and although they are not charged for any room and board, I believe they should still work even though it is only for their own self-satisfaction, sense of accomplishment, and pride in their own capabilities.

I want them to retain and practice their own religious and spiritual beliefs, and to encourage them to do this I make it a point to go to my own church every Sunday morning. Unfortunately, there is no Amish church out here, and it may seem somewhat incongruous that my going to my own church should make them better Christians in their own faith. But I learned, after my father died, that it is through the little things he and my mother did, and through their behavior in Life and from my observation of them, that they raised me to believe in the sense of decency and honor in which they believed and which was the code of their existence. For example, my father and mother would never permit my brothers and me to come to the dinner table without wearing a coat and tie. This taught us not be slobs, although at the time we could never understand that. So it is that I am hopeful that my going to church every Sunday (although, this is, mainly, because I have a deep and abiding faith in my own religious beliefs) will be somewhat of an example to these boys—if not now, perhaps later in life. I have learned that we all learn by the example of others who are close to us.

I hope Charles eventually will return to Pennsylvania and marry a nice Amish girl; and while this is what I want for him,

I believe the decision is his. Like you and your husband I can only stand by, give advice when I am asked for it, suffer with him when he makes his mistakes—and he will—and applaud him when he is successful: and hope, as he goes through all of this, that in time he will learn.

September 16, 1976

Thank you so much for your letter. It came at a time when a financial problem had arisen similar to that which you have discussed. A young friend of mine, gainfully employed, has asked me for money to pay a financial installment on the purchase of his car: his salary, apparently, not being sufficient to see him through to the end of the month. At least, that is the impression I have received. In these days of an inflated currency and growing inflation one finds many people in such a position.

Bill is a fine and decent hard-working young man. He has many qualities I admire, and for this reason alone I am going to decline to finance him. This might appear to be somewhat of a paradox, but in reality it isn't.

The possibility of using someone else as a crutch is a habit that is all too easy to develop. The welfare rolls are full of such people, and if a person is to develop self-reliance he must be discouraged from using other people as a crutch, no matter how mentally painful it might be to those who want to help him and have the financial means to do so.

All of us get into a financial bind at one time or another. That is, certainly, no disgrace, but it is a disgrace if we fail to honorably use our ingenuity to get ourselves out of it, or if we use such a situation to allow ourselves to become dependent upon our friends and family or upon society as a whole. We then become a leech. Considering the type of person Bill is, I am sure the situation will never come to this. He would never permit that for himself.

Bill, in essence, is quite similar to my father when he was a young man and attending Princeton University. And like myself, when I was at Georgetown, my father found himself an unwilling spectator at a race to see which would arrive first, the end of the check or the end of the month. If the end of the month arrived first all was well and good, but if the end of the check arrived first there was always the question of how to remain financially stable for the remainder of the month until the next monthly check arrived from home.

At that time, and through the remainder of his life, my father always wore a silver ring with a stone that was always a sapphire or resembled one. At such a time when insolvency was imminent he would go down to the local pawnbroker and pawn the ring for such a sum as would tide him over until he received his next monthly check. Then he would redeem his ring. This was the form of ingenuity he used to keep himself solvent at a time when he was a student, and I have never known a man who was more self-reliant than he was.

There are many people on welfare rolls today who could take a lesson from him and from a lot of other independent, self-reliant individuals. These are the people who built our country and people who have the qualities Bill has are among their number.

There is a saying that with age comes wisdom. I am not entirely certain that this is always correct because the infirmities of old age sometimes tend to cancel out wisdom, particularly if they are infirmities of the mind.

In the little village of Kragujevac in one of the Eastern European states lived an elderly gentleman whom I always respected and loved. The correspondence contained in the next several letters concerns him, a deeply religious man who, at this writing, has gone from us.

December 12, 1966

I know you are going to hate me for this, but I have brought you into a situation which I cannot control, and I think your family might be able to.

I received a letter from your uncle which leads me to believe he may have suffered a mental relapse. This is the only thing I can think from what has just happened. I am enclosing a copy of his letter to me and my reply to him. My reply to him and this letter to you are going out in the same mail.

What I actually think is that over the years he has had a very rough life, and that now, in his eighties, he is beginning to think back over the years before he entered the church, and that he has possibly reached a point of senility. I don't know; that is just what I think from what he said in his letter. I believe it is all in his own mind, and he probably doesn't even remember having written the letter.

I don't want to betray his confidence, but I feel you should be informed of this situation of you have not been as yet.

January 30, 1967

Thank you for your letter of the nineteenth

There is really nothing any of us can do about your uncle. The decision has to be his own, and while you and I may strongly disapprove, if he wishes to leave the church and marry, then it is his right to do so. I am going on the assumption he has not yet reached a point of senility, and he is going ahead on this with his eyes wide open.

I can see his point of view. He wants somebody to take care of him—not the state or a rest home, but some woman to look after him. The woman he has married probably has a home there in Kragujevac and may be relatively well settled. I don't really know. I am just guessing because I think that such a thing would have to be the case before he would ever consent to it. What I don't understand is why she would marry your uncle? He doesn't have a penny to his name; he's too old for sex; and I can't possibly think of any other reason why a woman would want to marry a man. Possibly she wants companionship (which may be the case with both of them), or if she is an aggressive woman, maybe she wants someone to dominate. Again, I don't know.

Actually, I don't think any of us should complain. It is his life, and if that's what he wants to do with it, who are you and I to try to stop him? After all, he's the one who has to live with the woman. You and I don't. If he brought her into your home and said, "We are moving in with you," that would be an entirely different matter. Then you'd have every right to raise hell. But as long as they do not interfere in your life or mine, neither of us has any right to do anything at all about it. The church might have that right, but not us. Indeed, there is nothing any of us can do about it.

In the late 1950s a young friend of mine was stationed at Luke Air Force Base just outside of Phoenix, Arizona. Eventually, his term of enlistment was at an end and he was honorably discharged from the service. He returned to his home on the east coast where, after a period of time he fell in love and was married.

I never saw him again, but we corresponded often. Then tragedy struck, and he went through a period of self-doubt and demoralization. The following correspondence refers to this.

May 20, 1964

I found your letter waiting for me when I returned from work this afternoon. I had not known about the divorce, nor that you have three children. Knowing you, I feel sure the children are most delightful, and it is a tragedy they are the innocent victims of a broken home.

From what you tell me about your wife (or former wife) I would judge her to be a very, very immature young woman. I should imagine, when she is older, she will deeply regret her precipitous action. It is, I know, quite a blow to be forced to accept, and I can understand why you would be heartsick about the whole thing. I have never suffered this particular type of body blow, but there have been many other setbacks in my private and personal life that have been just as serious and as frustrating to me as this is to you.

Of course, my friend, I can only judge from what you tell me in your letter, but what you don't say speaks volumes. Now, let's examine the situation. Having had twelve apartments in ten months would indicate that you are unhappy and dissatisfied and, above all, lost. Yet, I think, at the present time, as long as you retain the state of mind in which you probably find yourself you will be unhappy and dissatisfied and lost wherever you happen to be, whether it be in Malden or Phoenix or Timbuctoo.

It is true that the familiar sights and sounds of your present surroundings add to your present despondency, and this is understandable. Perhaps you should get away and go somewhere else. Then, too, if you do that you must remember this: that when you do you will preclude yourself from seeing your children, at least for the time you are gone from there. However, that can be only temporary. One thing I must impress upon you, and that is that wherever you go and whatever you do, you are going to have this feeling of emptiness and frustration until you come to grips with yourself and solve your personal problems. No one can do this for you but you yourself, and after you do that you will, I believe, find a degree of peace of mind.

How you are going to do it I do not know, nor will it be accomplished overnight. I know that time will help. So too can you. You must sit down with yourself and examine your problem for exactly what it is. Go over it with yourself thoroughly, everything that has happened to cause you all the mental anguish you are now undergoing. Ask yourself what there is that can be salvaged, if anything. When you have done that, you must ask yourself what you want for the future. You must lay out a definite plan or goal for your life that is well worthwhile for your economic, emotional, and spiritual well-being. Perhaps you will find that all of this can be accomplished where you are now. If so, all well and good. Perhaps you will discover that you can find your happiness away from Malden, where there are so many unfortunate memories. If so, then that is what you should do. But before you decide upon anything you must come to grips with yourself first.

March 1, 1966

Your unfinished letter of February 2 and the other one of the 22d reached me yesterday. I am glad you enclosed the unfinished one with the other because it tells me what you have been doing.

I am somewhat concerned about your own peace of mind, and I feel, from what you tell me in your letter, that you have been brooding so much about this divorce of yours you are making yourself very unhappy. You are transferring a guilt, which is not yours, to begin with, onto yourself, and you are carrying a load that you shouldn't carry at all. No matter what you may think at the moment, you didn't leave your wife; she left you. You may, perhaps, have performed the physical act of walking out when you discovered her unfaithfulness, but she left you even before that. She left you the moment she took a lover.

My friend, if, through the long years ahead, you are going to torture yourself unjustly by assuming a burden that is not yours, and that you cannot through your own endeavors throw off, perhaps you should obtain some professional assistance. A good psychologist might be able to render you some service.

This does not mean I believe you to be insane. Such is far from the case. You apparently have a problem that can affect your well-being, and since you cannot seem to throw it off by yourself, perhaps such professional help will assist you in doing so.

Twenty-five years or so ago I stood in need of doing the same thing. In fact, I was on the verge of a nervous breakdown. When I found out how much I would have to pay in order to have a nervous breakdown I decided I couldn't afford it, so I left Pennsylvania and tried to pull myself together under different surroundings. I was quite successful. These things are mostly always better if you can handle them by yourself. My difficulty was entirely different from yours, however, and what worked for me possibly would not work for you. Then, again, perhaps it would.

The news about your new job is most encouraging, and I am delighted to hear of it. This will, at least, keep you out of trouble.

I have found that life has a tendency to bring different things to different people. To me it has brought, among other things, the acquaintance of an Indian couple with several small children. The children are grown now, but while they were very young it was my pleasure to be in contact with their parents and even act as a surrogate father for one of the boys. The parents were of superior morality, industrious, and tried to do everything in their power to advance their children's welfare. Some of my correspondence with them follows.

October 10, 1969

Thank you for your letter of September 20. At the time it was written I had left for the Hawaiian Islands, so I did not receive it until just a few days ago. I am also grateful you enclosed Charles' spelling paper. He did very well on that, and I am quite proud of him. Apparently Charles is quite a scholar—at least, for the moment.

It would be wise, I think, to praise him when he does well and, if you are able to do so, to make a little something extra for him in the kitchen so that he will get the idea that you really are pleased with him and are proud of him. Also encourage him to do well when he doesn't, but don't push him too much, because if he is continually and too much criticized and nagged he may become so discouraged and rebellious as to give up entirely. He should be pushed just sufficiently for its purpose, and just how far this should be must depend upon your tactfulness and his attitude. For this purpose (if he needs pushing) you must set a temporary goal, but it must be a goal that he wants. Therefore, he must be the one who sets the goal he wishes to achieve, and if he does not do well you must push him gently and help him toward that goal, but no more than that.

Arithmetic is Charles' most important subject. In my opinion he should do as well or better in that than in any of his other subjects, although all of them are important. I know he has not yet reached the multiplication tables, but when he does (which will probably be when he gets to the third grade) he should know them through the twelve tables. He should know them so well that if he is asked what is 4 times 6, for example, he will be able to say 24 without even thinking about it. He should memorize all of them, and I know how best this can be accomplished.

When I was a small boy in elementary school I quite frequently did any number of things of which the teacher disapproved. The punishments they inflicted upon me and upon my classmates whenever they got out of line was to write the twelve tables or the four tables or the seven tables, or any of the others, five hundred times. Those teachers did me a favor, because by enduring my punishment I committed the multiplication tables to memory, and I have had no trouble with them at all.

I know I am speaking about studies that won't take place for a year or two, but if Charles does not commit the multiplication tables to memory he will never be able to do mathematics well for the rest of his life. I have seen it happen time and time again, and I know how important it is. And I know what I say is true. Charles should grow up to have an independent mind, but it should also be a disciplined mind, and memorizaiton is an excellent method to accomplish it. As a matter of fact, it would be good mental exercise for him to start now and learn some short poems or stories or sayings through memorization. It will certainly pay off in the long run over the years. Think about it.

November 28, 1971

I was somewhat distressed at the difficulty in which you found yourself when you were last here in Phoenix. I refer, of course, to the conference you had at the Indian School relative to your daughter who was in attendance there.

All children are rebels in one way or another, particularly at the age at which your daughter finds herself. I do not know the result of your conference, whether your daughter is still at the school or whether she has returned to her home with you. She is growing up, and the transition from childhood to maidenhood can be confusing and bewildering to a young girl. Definitely she needs counseling, but the counseling of a wise and understanding nature from an older woman whom she admires and trusts. That could be you, depending, of course, upon how close you and your daughter are to each other.

In a large number of cases, however, children do not confide in their parents to any great extent; rather, they restrict their confidences to people who are outside the family circle. This is unfortunate but it happens to be true—not in all cases, but in a large number of them. Whether or not it is true as appertains to your daughter I would have no way of knowing, but if she has found such a confidante or counselor in one of her teachers at the school. I would encourage the teacher to give that girl the guidance she needs. I would also point out to your daughter (tactfully and understandingly) that the course she has charted for herself will, in the long run, result in the loss of her own self-respect and in the respect of any and everyone else: that if she continues in that way of life she will, in all probability, end up by totally destroying herself morally and, possibly, physically.

I realize this whole subject is none of my business, but I make mention of these points in the hope that perhaps they might be of some value to you and because I happen to be Charles' foster father.

During the Second World War, I developed a number of friendships, but there was one that was more firm and more lasting than any of the others. He was my buddy all through training, and when we were sent our separate ways we kept in touch with one another. He entered college following the war years and, I'm afraid, almost burned himself out. He is now doing very well in his chosen field, but at that time it was touch and go. The letters following will show why.

April 26, 1949

Your letter arrived this morning shortly before I left for my noon class, and from the content of it I feel it should be answered right away.

To say the least, your change in plans is rather astonishing, but I can understand and do sympathize with your point of view. You must know that this is a very serious step you are planning to take, and you must be absolutely certain, before you take it, that you are no longer interested in becoming a physician. From the tone of your letter it appears to me you are very discouraged because you are not doing as well as you had hoped in organic chemistry and because you have not heard from the Medical School of the University of South Carolina.

You must remember that you alone are the only one who can decide what you want to do. You have been offered the prospects of a wonderful job, but there is no assurance you will receive it. You must take into consideration what will happen if you drop out of college and this job fails to materialize. You will be left without anything.

I realize, of course, that for the past three years you have put yourself through school and have, to a considerable degree, exhausted your own emotional stamina by continuing on during the summer at a relentless pace. I can understand under what a strain this has placed you, and I must say you certainly are to be admired for your tenacity.

Let us presume you have made up your mind that you do not wish to go to medical school, and you would like to concentrate on obtaining the position with Merrill Pharmaceutical Manufacturers Company. You say the gentleman who interviewed you was impressed that you had gone through college in three years. All of that is spendid. I am impressed too. But what is he and your future interviewers going to think when they learn you have not finished your formal education? If I were in his place I would say to myself that you were so anxious to get the job that you failed to finish the job you are now in; and that looks bad on any man's record. They will want a man who will finish his job and not stop when he is only one month away from his goal. You have worked for three years to obtain this college diploma. Don't throw it away when it is already within your grasp.

You say that organic chemistry is getting you down, that you are flunking it. Maybe you are and maybe you aren't. My opinion is that within the past three years you have had so much of it your stomach is turning over every time you see a test tube. But remember this: those men in Cincinnati will judge you not only on your appearance and your ability to sell but upon what you have accomplished. And if you let go now when you have only one month remaining of your school year they are going to take that into consideration. And when they do I wouldn't give you two cents for your opportunity of obtaining the position. Maybe I'm wrong. I don't know, but I think you should bend every effort to obtain your diploma by June, and then when you go to Cincinnati you will have something to show them. You will have accomplished a very great thing, and their respect for you and the influence you will be able to bring to bear upon them as a result of your accomplishment will add great weight to rendering their decision in your favor.

What you should do now is go to your adviser at the college. Tell him about your difficulties with organic chemistry and ask his advice. At the same time, even though it is coming out of your ears, even though you will never use it again, cram for that examination in organic chemistry. Go out and get drunk Saturday night. Get the whole thing out of your system for a day or so. Forget it over the weekend and have a wonderful time. Then, after you've done all that, go back and tackle the thing again. I know what I'm talking about.

August 22, 1949

Permit me, first of all, to offer my somewhat belated congratulations on your birthday, which occurred on August 8, but of which I was not aware until it was over.

You are probably going into the last phase of your summer-school course, if you have not already completed it, and your letter, which arrived Saturday, denotes a mood of distinct apprehension.

To put it quite bluntly, my friend, there must be some very definite reason why you are having such difficulty with organic chemistry. Possibly that difficulty lies in your hatred for the subject and, because of this hatred, you fail to work at it. I do not know. I am only surmising.

One thing is certain. You should take stock of yourself and

recognize the true reason why you are failing. It may be that you have developed a mental block against this particular subject. Then, if possible, eliminate this difficulty. I do not know what it is, but you yourself should know. I know that as far as you are concerned no words of mine can possibly make you like something you most cordially detest, but it appears to me you should make the best of a bad bargain (be it hatred of the course, hatred of the professor, or whatever reason) and work harder on this subject than any of the others you are taking. I will tell you this: there is no easy way out, as you are probably aware.

Naturally I am very sorry to receive this information about your studies in organic chemistry, and I know definitely there must be something wrong. I have full confidence in your abilities, and I know the reason is other than that you are unable to do the work. I remember when I was in college the registrar at the Georgetown University School of Foreign Service use to say to me: "David, if you like a course you will work at it very strongly, but if you don't like a course nothing I can say or anything any one this side of Hell can say or do will make you work." He was right, too.

September 11, 1949

Your telephone call yesterday came as a most pleasant surprise. It caught me a little off balance because I was rather at a loss to give a clear and concise recommendation to you right out of the blue sky without having much opportunity to think about it.

I really believe, though, that inasmuch as you are not certain as to what you wish to do it would be wise for you to return to college and pick up those eight credits that are necessary for you to graduate. At the same time I would get a job of some kind in the town where your college is located. With this I would also take a vocational-aptitude test at that college. This can be given to you by the man who is in charge of veterans' affairs at the college.

The test I have mentioned is given to determine an individual's aptitude for a particular field and to determine for what particular field an individual is best suited. I do, very strongly, recommend that you take this test. I am wrong when I use the singular here because it is a series of many tests, and while they will consume part of your time they are well worth it.

I think that at your age you should be doing something, and that is why I suggest that you obtain a job of some sort while you are finishing your college work. Some sort of bookkeeping job or handling accounts might be advisable inasmuch as you have had some sort of experience in that field while you were in the Merchant Marine. Any job will give you some valuable experience you can use later on because in it you can observe and learn something about the business of your employer.

As I mentioned to you on the telephone, if you decide to go to Guilford College, make certain from the registrar there that they are willing to transfer your credits to Charleston, and make certain from the registrar at Charleston that they are willing to accept them. You will be a candidate for graduation from Charleston and not from Guilford College.

Right now this is about all I can suggest to you until we find out how things are going to go in the future. Let's take one step at a time. The aptitude tests will take a period of several weeks before you will have completed them. When you do finish them let me know what the results are and then we will go on from there.

October 28, 1972

Dear Jim:

You cannot imagine with what pleasure I received your letter. I know, by this time, you have probably left the camp, but I was not aware of whether or not you would have changed your address at the college. I had thought about writing to you at this address, but then I thought No. I had better wait and see what my favorite young radical is up to and where he is doing it.

So you've fallen in love! Well, that's normal. She must be a very fine person to have you fall in love with her, because a person of your many excellent qualities and appreciation would pick only the best. Of course, I was somewhat mercurial when I was younger and it came to love. When I was seventeen I was in love with Mae West, and when I was in college I was in love with a new girl every week; but that probably isn't the same thing you are going through now.

Make certain, my son, that you love her for her spiritual and intellectual qualities as well as for her physical qualities. And don't do anything rash. You must recognize that there is a practical side to all of this as well as an emotional side. Should you marry you must remember you are taking on a very grave responsibility. That means, among other things, you are going to have to support her, and practically speaking, as far as I know you don't have two cents to rub together.

If you are not planning to marry at this time and are planning to live together (which my foster son is doing right now, and of which I strongly disapprove, not only for him but for you too) you should take precautions against the unexpected arrival of any children: at least, at this time. I do, however, want to pass on to you a few words my mother told me when I was nineteen years of age. She said, and I always remembered it because it is very sage advice: "David, you can always tell whether or not the girl with whom you have fallen in love is the one you should marry by asking yourself one question: Is this the girl I want to be the mother of my children?" I hope you will ask yourself the same question.

November 28, 1972

Dear Jim:

Somehow I feel sort of emptied. Where is that very nice, decent, clean-shaven, short-haired young man named Jim who accompanied me to Vancouver? He's gone! And while I sit here and realize he's never going to return I must get use to this new Jim who is living in sin with his girl. I agree with your young lady's family. I do not and cannot approve of this any more than I approve of it with my own foster son here in Phoenix, who was living with his girl until she moved to El Paso to attend a school of nursing there. Eventually they too intend to be married.

There is one thing which you both probably do not realize and which, possibly, has never occurred to you. That is, without realizing it, you could be contributing to her eventually becoming a harlot. I know these words will be somewhat of an affront to you and to the young lady, and, I assure you, my young friend, this is not the way I intend them. But I believe if you will stop and think about it for a few minutes you will come to the same conclusion to which I have come: that such a possibility does exist.

Suppose you both decide that because of the difference in your temperaments marriage would not be a suitable arrangement and you decide to part. You go your way and the girl, eventually, falls in love with another boy, and the same arrangement is made. Again both decide it is an erroneous arrangement and there is another parting. There could be a third and even a fourth, and each time the girl does this she is cheapening herself in the eyes of her contemporaries. The boy does not cheapen himself. It is only the girl who does. There are very few boys who are interested in marrying a girl who has been living with a series of men, or sometimes even just one.

Now, this doesn't mean that your young lady is going to do all of this or have all of this happen to her. In all probability it won't happen to her at all, but given the proper circumstances occurring at the proper time, it could happen.

Jim, my son, I believe what you and this young lady are doing is wrong. One either accepts the responsibility of marriage or one does not. You would be right, of course, in telling me it is none of my business, but for your sake and for hers I hope you will both reconsider what you are doing.

January 27, 1976

Dear Jim:

Jim, it is about time! You should have been married when you decided to cohabitate, and a feeling of shame should exist for what you have been doing since that time and what you are and will be doing between now and next March.

In my opinion you and Dorothy are wrong about your marriage. You cannot have it your own way, because it is not your wedding. You and Dorothy are only the bride and groom. The only function you two have is to get married. That is all. It is not even your parents' wedding, Jim. Their function is to supply you, and that is all they do. The wedding belongs to Dorothy's mother and father. They are the ones who will pay for it. They decide who is going to be invited to the wedding, not you. They will ask your parents for a list of guests whom your parents would like to have invited, and they will ask you for your list, too. It will be very tactful for you to ask Dorothy to ask her parents how big a list your parents and you should submit. This can be a rather tricky affair, particularly if Dorothy's parents do not have sufficient funds to give a large wedding and reception. I do not know whether they do or not, but it would still be a tactful thing for you to do.

Please remember that you and Dorothy have caused your parents and hers to go through a living hell because you both insisted on living together outside the laws of the church and the mores of society. By doing this you have caused them embarrassment in front of their friends and acquaintances because they are of a generation that look with abhorrence upon the questionable morality you both embrace. This wedding is something both sets of parents have been looking forward to ever since you and Dorothy showed an interest in one another. After all that has been done it would be very unfair for the two of you to deprive them of participation in the arrangements and planning of your wedding. When you have a daughter and she turns eighteen or twenty, then it will be your wedding. In the meantime, let them have theirs now.

Jim, you have had everything your own way up to now. Please don't do anything that will hurt your parents .

June 7, 1965

Dear Carlos:

Your most welcome letter reached me a few minutes ago. I was most shocked to hear of the interest rate you will have to pay for a mortgage for your new house. Seven percent is an exorbitant rate of interest. However, I can readily understand why, with money in scarce supply, this should be the case.

Since you are planning to build a home, you undoubtedly already own a piece of land on that island of yours. Hang on to it, but don't build yet. Money is not always going to be in short supply nor is the layoff at the oil company going to last forever. From what you tell me, as far as money is concerned, you are in the middle of a seller's market. Just sit tight for the time being. Don't build now.

I haven't the remotest idea where this land of yours is located. Since you want to build a home on it, the land is undoubtedly in a residential area. Then again, it may not be. Depending upon the location of the land, I would for the time being try to lease the land to someone so that you will have an income coming in from that source. Have you had a geological survey made of the land to discover whether or not there is oil under it? If you lease the property, it can give you a start toward a business of your own; which is what you really want.

Of course, I am groping in the dark, so to speak, when I mention all of this to you. There are so many things I do not know. One thing I would not do is to become discouraged and pick up stakes and go somewhere else. I would only do that as a last resort. After all, your home is on the island of Curaçao, and you are well known there. In Venezuela you would be just another foreigner trying to make a living while, at the same time, fighting the prejudices that the native-born population of any country has against foreigners for one reason or another, and financially encumbered with a wife and child. If you do decide to move, please consider, before you make the move, that you must have contacts in the country to which you are moving. You should not go there blind—that is, without having prearranged interviews for the prospect of employment. And if you go, go alone the first time. Put your wife and child with her family or yours, because then your expenses will be only one third as much as they would be if you took them with you. Find out, first of all, whether or not you are going to like it. If you think you will, get settled and send for your family.

But, as I said, I would not make this move unless I felt it was absolutely necessary to do so, unless I was completely certain there would be no opportunities available to me in Curaçao. Yet I cannot believe that such is the case with you. I am sure you have many opportunities remaining. All it needs is a little imagination on your part. I know that if I owned land in Curaçao I would exploit it to the fullest extent. Here is how I would do so: First of all, I would survey the economic situation as it exists. There is the oil company. This I have already mentioned. Second, you are right in the middle of the biggest tourist boom in the history of the Caribbean. New hotels and tourist resorts are going up throughout the entire area. This means that new business will be coming in, and if I am correct, the price of land is going to go up. The layoff of the oil workers is only one phase of your economy. If you look at it in an optimistic manner and if you play your cards right, that land of yours could possibly be the foundation for your fortune.

Knowing the economy of your island far better than I do, you can probably think of many other things. I have mentioned just two. There is no question at all but that you have to have a stake before you can do anything. Your stake is that land of yours, if you will think things out for yourself and do so intelligently with an eye to the future. Survey the economic growth and the needs of your area, and find out how you can use it to your greatest advantage. It will require intelligence, daring, and imagination. Depending upon what you do and how you do it, you can make yourself a fortune or you can lose your shirt. But no man ever obtained anything for himself just by sitting still and doing nothing. If you're going to get your own business you've got to take a chance. This, I think, you know anyway.

Part III

HISTORY AND POLITICS AND WAR

August 17, 1968

Dear Carlos:

Your letter arrived while I was in Mexico deep-sea fishing. It was very nice to hear from you, and I will endeavor to answer your questions concerning the integration problem in the United States.

To understand the problem one has to go back to approximately the year 1640, when the Dutch slavers landed the first slaves on the North American continent. That act began the slave trade in this country. It existed throughout the entire length and breadth of the Colonies, and it was only when the North discovered it was economically unsound for the North to have slavery that they (the North) did away with it. At that time the situation held true in the South, but the invention of the cotton gin in the South made slavery economicallly feasible. That is the reason why the South held to slavery while the North abjured it. Believe me, if the North could have made a profit from slavery, they would have held on to it too. But the fact was that the North considered it an economic loss to retain slavery, and that is why, among other reasons, the North proclaimed the moral concept of the evils of slavery. Since the institution was not economically feasible for them they opposed it on the moral concept that no man should own slaves as property or have the right to deprive another of his freedom. But this, at the beginning, was a minor difference between the North and the South. The real difference was economic and political—a question of whether or not the states should rule themselves or the federal government should rule the states—and that battle is still going on.

There is no more slavery in this country. That question was

decided a hundred years ago, and throughout this country one has become accustomed to the idea of the Negro as an independent being. During the period of the occupation of the South by northern troops just after the surrender of Lee at Appomattox, many of the wives of the northern officers who came to the South to be with their husbands wanted white Scotch girls to be nurses for their children. They wouldn't accept the colored "mammys" the southern ladies had for their children. In other words, what I am saying is that the South knew and understood the Negro race but the North didn't. This hypocritical farce has been going on for over a century. The North won't accept the Negro as an equal any more than the South will.

Now, down on that island of yours you cannot understand this because you have never undergone the trial and turmoil of a civil war such as we have undergone, and you cannot understand the background and hatred that has existed (and, in many cases, is still existing) since 1640.

It is true that these people are American citizens and as such are entitled to every protection under the law. But what every foreigner seems to be unable to understand is the background of the problem. In a brief word, the background is this: They are not always accepted, and you cannot pass a law requiring one person to like another person. In essence, that is what the present Civil Rights Law tries to do. The Negro race wants the integration of schools and public facilities, and to this they are entitled. No one denies that. This is as it should be. But many want more. Many want and expect acceptance through social intercourse. In numerous cases you will find that this is denied among the Caucasians themselves and among the Negroes themselves. I am sure, in Curaçao there are many members of your own race with whom you would rather not associate, and the same is true not only in this country but throughout the world. As I have said, they want to be liked. They are not alone; everyone does. But no law can be passed that will accomplish this. This is the reality of the situation.

You have heard of the riots that have been going on it New

York, Jersey City, Rochester, and a few other places. Your own innate intelligence will cause you to look and see what caused these riots. You will see that every single one of them was started because the police arrested a Negro for doing something that was illegal. Then the riots started, and the Negroes claimed police brutality. I cannot believe there was much of that. What were the police supposed to do? Let the Negroes rape, riot, and look the other way when they did? What would you have done if someone came after you with a razor or a knife? Wouldn't you have defended yourself?

The Negroes are hurting themselves by this rioting. And you will notice that a vast majority of this rioting is taking place in northern and not southern cities: in the North, which is supposed to be the friend of the Negro. The bitter resentment that has risen because of these riotings may well have a bearing on the presidential election which is coming up in November. Also, one of the things you probably do not know is that none of the responsible leaders of the Negro movement condones these riots. And I have been advised that the Federal Bureau of Investigation has proof that these riots are fomented by communist elements within the Negro ranks.

I have given you a background and an opinion. I do not know what you think of it. Certainly it is not the end of the road for either black or white, and it is certain to go on. But, when you judge us, put yourself in our place. Judge us by facts, not emotions. If you know the facts ask yourself how you would react, knowing our history and our background. I don't apologize for any of it. Perhaps I should, but I know the background, so I don't.

September 21, 1964

Dear Carlos:

I was most interested in your letter. The question of the Negro situation in the United States is one of exceptional complexity. You have undoubtedly read in your newspapers of the riots that have been taking place throughout the North and the South. I do not know how your newspapers have slanted them, but these riots, actually, have nothing do with the question of the rights of the Negro race. They have been started by hoodlums and engaged in by hoodlums in complete violation of law and order. They cannot be and are not condoned by the responsible members of the white and Negro communities.

Last week there was a strike or boycott of various white families against the New York City School Board. This was not a boycott against segregation or even for it. It was not a question of whether or not Negroes should attend the public schools of New York City. This was a question of whether or not white children, and the colored children too, should be forced to leave their neighborhood schools to attend schools in another part of the city in order for integration to be accomplished in those schools.

The right of the Negro to attend the schools of New York is not in question. Up until this whole mess started, the Negroes, living in one section of New York attended the schools located in that section. In fact, anyone living in any section of the city attended the school in the section in which he lived. If someone, white or colored or anything else, moved to another section of the city, the children would attend the school in the section into which they had moved. It didn't make any difference if a child was black or white or even green. That Negroes tend to live in one particular section of the city automatically created a de facto segregation, but that is not the fault of the school board or the fault of anyone else. The courts want to overcome this by forcing both white and colored families to remove certain of their children from the neighborhood schools they had been attending and require them to attend schools in neighborhoods of a different ethnic background, which are often miles distant from their homes. This was to be done by busing and for the purpose of creating integrated schools.

In my opinion, and in the opinion of a number of other people, the courts have overstepped their authority by ordering busing. The power to make this decision belongs to the state legislatures, not to the judiciary, and the usurpation of this power by the judiciary is patently unconstitutional and therefore illegal.

September 30, 1957

Dear Carlos:

You have undoubtedly been reading in your newspapers and elsewhere concerning the internal difficulties that are in progress here in the United States, particularly in the State of Arkansas. It is very unfortunate that erroneous opinions seem to be getting into the newspapers of other countries regarding this difficulty, which is one peculiar to the United States of America.

As you are aware, the United States have several minority groups within our borders. One of these is the Negro race. Following the Civil War this race was freed from the bonds of slavery and given citizenship. That is as it should be, but among the people of our country there are very deep divisions just as there are among the people of other countries. We also have a government which, in theory, at any rate, is supposed to be subservient to the authority of the several states. That is, our Founding Fathers set up our Constitution so that our government would be a government of independent sovereign states, and the federal government should have only such power as should be surrendered to it by the states. That was the idea. Since the year 1789 the federal government has continually encroached more and more upon the authority of the state governments until, by now, it has grown dangerously powerful.

The matter of the public schools in the United States is a local matter in which the federal government has no authority either by law or by custom. This is part of the internal affairs of each state. The actual question is not one of whether or not Central High School in Little Rock, Arkansas, should have segregation or integration (Caucasian and colored children attending the same school) but whether or not the federal government has the right to intervene in the affairs of the several states. It is a legal question, and the sending of troops into a sovereign state, such as President Eisenhower has done, is in my opinion a violation of the rights and prerogatives of the sovereign states. There are other ways, legal, rather than extra-legal, by which the question of integration can be resolved. The use of this method is not one of them.

I admire President Eisenhower a great deal. He has done much for this country and for the people of the world, but no man is infallible, and in this instance I believe he was ill-advised.

In many ways the question of integration is merely symbolic of the real difficulty, which is the power of the federal government as opposed to the rights of the states under the Constitution.

December 23, 1947

Dear Vittorio:

I heard over the radio last evening that the Italian Legislative Assembly has passed a new constitution for Italy that forever bans the monarchy from returning. Of course, my friend, I know you are a conservative Republican, and, it is therefore with hesitancy that I mention that I cannot believe this will last. The course of past history has proved that, sooner or later, Italy will return to her monarchy: possibly not retain it forever, but until such time as she is able to discard it without injury to her traditions and institutions.

You see, the reality of a people to rule themselves is not always possible. If you doubt that, look at the Russians. A nation that has been under one form or system of government for centuries cannot, with one stroke of a pen, change that government. Italy was under a monarchy even prior to the days of the Unification Movement under Mazzini and Cavour. Since Italy has been under the rule of the Bourbons, the Hapsburgs, the House of Savoy, the House of Bourbon Parma and others, she has developed institutions and traditions that are peculiar to monarchy, and these cannot be thrown off all at once. If they decay at all it will be gradually over a period of decades and centuries.

The result of the present action will be, I believe, a period of confusion and chaos which may lead to a return of constitutional monarchy, not under Vittorio Emmanuel III nor under Umberto, but under Umberto's son, the Prince of Naples. Then, under a constitutional monarchy you will not only have a symbol of order and authority, but Italy will be able gradually to work out her destiny under a constitutional government through the medium of representative institutions with which Italy has been unfamiliar for many centuries.

It may be I am wrong. It may be that the assistance the United States is rendering your country may have some influence for order and stability. It is possible that this influence may extend the growth of your republic. I do not know. I feel, however, that no nation is ready for self-government until the people of that nation have sufficient education in the art of self-government to attempt it. To do otherwise will lead to disorder, chaos, and gradual dissolution.

August 3, 1950

Dear Elsie:

Looking into my files I find the last letter I addressed to you was in October of last year; and yet, two unanswered letters of yours remain on my desk. How rude and inconsiderate you must believe me to be for neglecting my friendship for you so lengthily.

The Korean War is an unpleasantness that has all of us upset because there is no one of us who knows whether he will be called to active duty in the military service of our nation. That could very well be. Right now my future and that of many of my compatriots seem to hinge upon the progress of our armed forces on that peninsula, and as you know, and as I have known, we have been consistently losing the war up to now. I feel it will be continued, at least until it is won by us, and that it is going to take a long, long time to accomplish this.

It appears that the United States Government has acted very foolishly in cutting down on its military strength both at home and abroad. There are, I believe, individuals in the Department of Defense who are inimical to our American heritage and way

of life; also in the Department of State. How else can one rec-
oncile the foolish and inane foreign policy of the United States
in Asia; the do-nothing policy of the United States in China
while the communist hordes swept through and overran that
country; the diplomatic surrender of President Roosevelt to Pre-
mier Stalin at Yalta; and the haphazard, grudging support for the
government of the Emperor Bao Dai in Indochina? Do you
realize that in the last military appropriation made for stopping
the spread of Communism ten billion dollars was earmarked for
South Korea? Of that entire sum South Korea received only two
hundred dollars because the State Department of my country felt
that the South Koreans would use the weapons they received from
the United States to attack and fight the North Koreans. A vast
number of my countrymen are wondering who, in the United
States Department of State, is responsible for this situation and
why it was permitted to occur. We may never know. Scandals
like that seldom break, and even when they do they are very
quickly hushed up. You can rest assured that when the next
election comes my vote will be cast against the candidates of the
political party that, at present, is in control of our government.

I see I have gone on at great length concerning the political
situation here in the United States. Possibly I should not have
criticized my government to one who is not an American citizen.
Yet it is only through criticism and discussion we can learn and
evaluate. I love my country very much, but I believe that our
economic and our social independence, both individually and
collectively, are being insidiously threatened by external and internal sources. And I believe that the most dangerous of these is
the internal source.

July 17, 1954

Dear Tommy:

The world situation has been much on my mind of late.
Indeed, I would presume it has been much on the mind of a great
many people.

I have been particularly concerned over the results of the failure of the Geneva Conference. In the meantime I have received a letter from the former Chancellor of Germany, Herr Franz von Papen, in which he gives me his views relative to the stability of Europe. Herr von Papen's letter was addressed to me on June 29th, and he wrote the following:

"Meanwhile, we are in much the same situation: whether to be able to avoid a third world war or not! We are, over here, not yet informed about the outcome of Churchill's and Eden's visit and whether the grave differences with the policies of your country may have been settled. I doubt it. You can't recognize Red China and drop Formosa. It would mean to give up your strongest point in the whole Pacific defense line and to leave the southern flank of Japan in the mash.

"What price will be asked for an armistice in Indochina? Certainly the recognition of Peking and the renuciation of Germany to be rearmed. France would be glad to give in on both points, but I suppose you could, perhaps, swallow the first—not the second. It would upset your whole strategic plan.

"So, the 20th of July may create a very dangerous situation. It is a pity that the only feasible policy—a separation of the Chinese from the Soviet Bloc—could not be designed. Its supposition will be that the area of colonization in Asia (and everywhere) have ended once and for all. I am convinced of the possibility to develop a sort of Communism in China similar to 'Titoism'—and free from Soviet leadership. But what about Hong Kong etc. and Africa? I am hoping with you that your government may use your old friendship with France to aid them in finding the right way out of this impossible vacuum."

I am afraid I cannot agree with all Herr von Papen has to say relative to a Communist China as distinct from Soviet Russia, but on most other points of his letter I am in agreement.

There are many people who will tell you that we are living today in a state of wary and uneasy peace. Yet I cannot feel that this is altogether true. I believe that whether we like it or not, the world is at war and has been since 1914; that whether we like it or not we are engaged in a Second Hundred Years War, the outcome of which may not be seen in your lifetime or mine. It is a very subtle conflict because it is not a struggle of principality against principality, but is a conflict of ideologies, of two entirely different ways of life that are incompatible with one another: a struggle between two civilizations, both of which have had their origin in Europe, and one of which has been embraced and given substance by the oriental mind.

It is not beyond peradventure of a doubt to believe that this Second Hundred Years War has been and is divided into a variety of phases. The first phase appears to have lasted from 1914 through 1918, the second phase from 1919 through August of 1939, the third phase from September of 1939 through 1945, the fourth phase from 1946 to June of 1950, and the fifth phase from June of 1950 to and including the present. The struggle, thus far, has encompassed all but the first decade of our twentieth century, and I believe it will extend a great deal further.

Phase One of the conflict saw a cascade of thrones in Europe. The monarchy, as a governing institution, ceased to exist in Germany, Austria, Russia, and a number of other European sovereignties. It also saw an attempt to establish a Communist regime in Hungary (which failed) and a successful attempt to establish it in Russia. The attempt to do the same in Germany also failed.

Here (in Russia) the struggle, which had been going on under the surface for so many years, ever since the proclamation of the Communist Manifesto in 1848 by Karl Marx and Friedrich Engels, was able to come to the surface and, taking advantage of a weakened and exhausted Europe, seize the Government of Russia and almost seize that of Germany. Although the Communist regimes in Hungary and German were stamped out, the allied attempt in 1919 to do the same in Russia and Siberia resulted in a dismal failure. Phase One of the conflict appears to have ended there.

In the meantime, Communism grew and prospered. By 1939 it had flared up in Spain; it had seized the Baltic States and Poland. By 1945 it had swept over the Balkan States and firmly entrenched itself in half of Europe. In the Far East Communism proceeded unopposed in China by the Western World and, indeed, in many instances with the West's tacit approval and connivance.

Phase Five began with the advent of the Korean War. It is still in progress, but it might have ended some time ago if General Douglas MacArthur had been permitted to bomb and strafe the enemy installations and his logistical support that lay in the Manchurian sanctuary beyond the Yalu. But this was not permitted, and the United Nations were forced to fight a limited and delaying action that could only lead not to ultimate victory but to a stalemate, thus permitting the Communist armies of China to build up their military potential north of the Yalu and, after signing an armistice, hold ready those armies that had fought against the United Nations in Korea for use against the forces of the Western Powers in Indochina, Malaya, Burma, and Southeast Asia generally.

The Western World must regard the fact that we have been consistently losing the battle against Communism. The stalemate in Korea, the disaster at Dien Bien Phu, the systematic evacuation of the Hanoi-Haiphong salient in Indochina and the Red River Delta Region, give evidence of this fact as plainly as does the disunity that exists among the Western Powers. Only a strong, united Western World opposed to Communism can halt that ideology in its tracks, and that we do not have. We must remember that France is no longer a first-rate power. We must remember that England is fearful of a hydrogen bomb being implanted upon her shores, and we must remember that upon neither of these nations, individually, can we depend for support in the event of a conflict with the Soviet Union. In Western Europe we must depend upon a NATO Alliance that has Western Germany as its focal point. In the Near East we depend upon Turkey and an understanding with the Mohammedan-Moslem nations, if that can be achieved. India in Central Asia is our weakest link, and in the Far East we must secure a pact with Japan, Australia, New Zealand, and the other noncommunist Southeast Asian states.

I had not meant to lecture to you about a subject concerning which you are, undoubtedly, far better acquainted than I. It is just that it is a subject upon which I feel so strongly. Unless we possess unity of purpose among the nations of the Western World, I greatly fear we are going to continue losing the war against Communism as we are doing now.

March 31, 1960

My Dear Colonel:

First of all, permit me to thank you for your prompt response to my letter and for the enclosures you sent me. These are exactly what I want. I have taken a little time to make up my mind concerning the color scheme, but I sent them off to the Donegal Carpet Company yesterday. All I have to know now is how much they are going to charge me for manufacturing a carpet such as I have in mind and probably can't afford.

You are perfectly right in everything you have said concerning Khrushchev's visit to Paris. But after reading the newspapers of the past several weeks, what I cannot understand is the attitude of my own government. It appears to me, and to a good many Americans, that following the British line of ceasing atomic tests without an ironclad guarantee of inspection is nothing less than appeasement of the Russians. I should think that the British would have learned their lesson in 1938 when Prime Minister Chamberlain met with Daladier and Hitler and Mussolini at Munich. We all know what happened there, and it seems to me, we are repeating that same folly. No, you are perfectly correct. The Russians understand nothing but strength, and if we must negotiate at all we must negotiate through strength. An appeaser once said: "I would rather be Red than dead." Personally, I would rather be dead than Red. I think the vast majority of America feels as I do.

At the present time we are in the opening stages of our national election. As you are probably aware I am a member of the Republican Party as opposed to the principles of the Democratic Party. I believe the election this year will be fought on two issues. The first one and, primarily, the most important will be foreign policy, and the second one will probably be the farm issue. Who the Democratic candidate will be I do not know. It is quite possible it will be Adlai Stevenson. Vice President Nixon will, undoubtedly, win the Republican nomination, but oddly enough, there seems to be some small opposition developing. The opposition seems to be crystallizing around Senator Barry Goldwater of Arizona. A few days ago the Republican Party in South Carolina instructed its delegates to cast their ballots for Senator Goldwater for President. What our delegation from Arizona will do at the national convention in Chicago we do not know. Senator Goldwater is conservative in his thinking and believes in negotiation through strength. There is a strong feeling of conservativism sweeping the nation just now, and Senator Goldwater is, more or less, the spokesman for this. He would make an excellent president, but I feel that this year the senator is not sufficiently strong to obtain sufficient votes of the delegates to capture the nomination.

Since the banishment of the Royal Family, Yugoslavia has been an unhappy country. Under a Communist regime freedom has been suppressed, and the right to private property has been negated. A friend of mine, an intellectual, who was studying in the United States, was not happy about it either. His comments to me led to my reply.

August 9, 1962

I was happy to receive your letter a few minutes ago, and I am writing immediately to give you what I believe to be the answers to some of the questions you have asked.

First of all, permit me to thank you for the very lovely hand-carved salad set you sent me, and also for the two small dolls dressed in native Yugoslav costume. It was very kind of you to think of me, and totally unexpected. I want to send you some of the things we have here in the West, so if you will write to me and tell me your shirt size, that is, the size of the collar and the sleeve, I will be able to do so. I think you will find them useful.

You say you wish to stay in the United States. I assume you mean permanently. If such is the case the reasons you have for wanting to stay here are paramount. If you wish to escape from Communism and all that it means and stands for, and assume the status of a refugee from Communist Yugoslavia, and you are sincere in this, I would recommend that you go privately to the Philadelphia Office of the Federal Bureau of Investigation and tell them you do not wish to return to Communist Yugoslavia, and ask for asylum in this country.

You will be asked a great number of questions because the Federal Bureau of Investigation will want to determine (1) whether or not you are a spy planted here by the Communists; (2) whether or not you want to live in this country just because you prefer it to your own; (3) whether or not you are in danger of your life if you return to your country; and (4) whether or not you are sick and tired of the Communist system and are using this means to escape from it.

Understand, at the same time, that if you do this thing, your wife and your mother may suffer as a consequence because they are back there in Yugoslavia, and at the moment, there is no way in the world for them to get out. If they are not arrested as a result of your actions in this respect, rest assured they will be very closely watched, and their lives will probably be made a living hell. As I understand it, your mother is visiting your sister right now somewhere in Austria. If your sister would invite your wife to visit her right now, then your mother and your wife would both be out of the country, and you could proceed with this plan without endangering either of them. The decision is yours.

Now, as to your other statement concerning your remaining in the United States for a year: This is a matter that will have to be handled by the State Department and your own government. Knowing the nature of Communism, as I have reason to know it, I would regretfully suggest that if your government becomes aware of your desire to remain in the United States for even just a year, they would be inclined to suspect your loyalty and would call you back to Yugoslavia immediately. I also suggest that it would be a very long time, if ever, before you would be permitted to leave your country again. I may be wrong, but that is what I think would happen. If you were called back and you did not apply for asylum there is nothing this country could do to prevent it. That is my advice to you. I must warn you, though, that any inquiries you make must be of the most cautiously discreet kind so that they do not come to the ears of your government either here or in your own country. If you are in any way indiscreet you may have reason to suffer for it.

Again, my thanks for your very nice gift.

After the debacle at Dien Bien Phu the defense of Southeast Asia against the inflow of Communist aggression passed to the United States. Not only were American Advisors sent to assist the South Vietnamese, but American troops as well. Among them was a young Marine Corps sergeant from Illinois whose correspondence was always a source of pleasure.

January 8, 1970

I must apologize to you for a rather long delay in my correspondence. Shortly after I received your last letter I left for Pennsylvania to visit with my mother and my brothers and sister and their families over the Christmas holidays. Like an idiot I forgot to take anyone's address with me, so I couldn't write to any of the people I really wanted to write to while I was there.

I arrived in Phoenix about eleven o'clock Monday evening after a rather ghastly trip through an abominable weather picture of snow and, in some cases, near-blizzard conditions. And I had to hurry because of the cargo I was carrying. As I probably told you, my brother has a brewery which is the oldest one in the United States that has been in continuous operation in the same family since 1829. I brought back six cases of beer. My brother tells me that beer freezes at a temperature of 27 degrees. Wherever I stopped for the night the temperature was well below that, but I was able to put the car in the hotel garage rather than leave it out. That is, except for Monday night. I drove from Oklahoma City, and I usually stop for the night at Alburquerque, but it was three o'clock in the afternoon when I arrived there, so I thought I would go on to Gallup. I arrived there about five-thirty, and the temperature for that night was predicted to be in the low teens, and I figured I could make Phoenix by ten-thirty that night, so I just came on. Besides, there wasn't any place I could put the car without leaving it outside. I mean, if I had stayed that night in Gallup. In many ways driving directly from Oklahoma City to Phoenix was a damned stupid thing to do because that distance is about one thousand miles, and I was by myself, and I had no one to spell me at the wheel.

Since I have been back things have been quiet, and I have been trying to get settled again. Your letters, my friend, are very interesting, and I have been reading over the last one you wrote. What you do is of interest to me, and, I suppose, in a certain sense, it is to you too, because it means your survival. But like yourself, I am looking forward to the time when you can come home. That shouldn't be too long now.

The one thing that gets my goat about this war is that we do not finish it off. I for one am all in favor of using all the power we possess—to go north and clean up that place and to put an end to this nonsense once and for all. But I am afraid mine is one of the few voices left that is crying in the wilderness, and a loud and very vocal minority of draft dodgers, society dropouts, and other ill-assorted groups who want all of the privileges of citizenship and none of the responsibilities attendant to them seem to have the ears of the politicians. Nothing comes easy, and it gets me furious when I see wonderful people like yourself and your companions laying your lives on the line so that the misbegotten misfits in our society can spit, stamp upon, and burn our country's flag while flying the flag of our enemy. Even as I write this, my friend, I can feel my temper rising, so I had better finish this letter and give myself some time to calm down.

March 9, 1966

Dear Tommy:

It has been some time since your letter arrived at my desk. I was in Pennsylvania when it reached Phoenix, and later that same month I left for London. I was only gone for a short time and spent about a week in England, where I managed to buy an eighteenth-century painting I am having hung in my living room, and where I met and entertained and was entertained by some friends of mine over there. It was a most delightful week, but I am very glad to be home.

A letter arrived from a young friend of mine, a sergeant in the United States Marine Corps stationed at Danang in Vietnam. He told me what he could of the fighting going on there. It must be a regular hell-hole, with the mosquitoes and the mud and the generally unhealthy climate. But I admire the sergeant, and I admire every one of those boys who are over there. The reason why they are there is very simple although it doesn't seem to penetrate the simple-minded brains of the left-wing element of this country. If we don't fight now we will be fighting later, and closer to our own home shores. In fact, we should have done our fighting long ago before the menace became as bad as it is. It should have been done by the Allied Powers in 1919 with the occupation of Archangel when we had an opportunity to kill Communism in its cradle in Russia. But, no! At that time it was a question of too little too late. Now look at the mess we're in. Every time we started to do anything it was always a question of too little too late. I hope this time we intend to follow through.

By this time you should be quite recovered from your automobile accident. It is unfortunate you were injured. I hope you had sufficient insurance to cover medical and hospital or doctors' costs that may have resulted from it.

I think one of the worst drivers with whom I have ever driven is a Portuguese taxi driver in Lisbon. They all seem to drive alike. Also, in Santo Domingo the drivers act as though they have just received a new toy. They are constantly honking their horns, and when they come to an intersection they seem to close their eyes and go full speed ahead praying that nothing is coming from the other direction. Why there aren't more accidents I cannot understand.

One of the most idealistic and charming people I have ever known was a Greek Orthodox priest who did yeoman work in a small Yugoslav village. Idealism, however, is not always a practical and workable philosophy to follow, and what we might prefer to have or to do does not always relate satisfactorily to a given situation as it actually exists.

June 11, 1956

My many thanks to you for your letter of May 31. I read it with a great deal of interest, particularly your suggestion of a political union of the states of the Western Hemisphere. While such a step would appear logical in theory, it would undoubtedly be unworkable in fact. There are many ethnic as well as nationalistic and cultural reasons why such a union would be inadvisable.

Ethnically, we are an Anglo-Saxon people, and the nations south of us are Latins. Both we and they have different political and cultural heritages. The Latin Americans have developed a paternalistic system of government that is based upon the paternalistic systems of government in Spain and in Portugal and which is still existent there today. We have developed along entirely different lines.

Economically, if we were to be united politically with them, it would mean that the transit barriers between us and them would no longer exist, and they would come to this country in droves because we have a much higher standard of living than they have, and they could make much more money up here.

All of this would not only deprive the American employee of jobs but would tend to reduce the wage scale in the United States because those people would be willing to work at what we would regard as starvation wages, against the American worker who would be unable to compete.

This is not a fantasy. This we have found out to be true. During the 1930s and the 1940s a great many of the very poor people of Puerto Rico came to the United States in great numbers, and they built up quite a colony of Puerto Ricans in New York City. They were able to come because of the peculiar relationship that exists between the United States and Puerto Rico. The Puerto Ricans are regarded as United States citizens and, as such, they are permitted free entry into the continental United States.

They came to New York and settled there and applied for financial relief from the State of New York. Since they had become citizens (or residents) of the State of New York they became eligible for state welfare, and the State of New York had to pay them a great deal of money for their financial relief, and this amount was far more than any of them had ever seen in Puerto Rico. The result is that today New York has a very large number of Puerto Ricans living off the taxpayer, and the taxes the New Yorker has to pay to support these people are tremendous.

Both economically and politically I am afraid the United States would be the loser in such a program as you mention. I am afraid I cannot agree with you that this is the wisest course for us to take.

One of the most intelligent men I know is a retired colonel of the Spanish army. He is a noted historian in his own right. It has always been a pleasure to exchange views with him.

March 10, 1958

There are two letters on my desk from you (January 11th and February 1st) which I have been so rude as not to answer. I do owe you my sincere apologies for my bad manners.

As you have observed in a card you have addressed to me, we have finally sent a satellite orbiting into space. It is about time! I, and a majority of my countrymen, are deeply embarrassed and ashamed that our officials in charge of this program saw fit to procrastinate, thus permitting the Russians the propaganda victory they achieved through the launching of their satellite.

To us the launching of the Soviet satellite was more than just a propaganda victory for the Russians. To us it was, actually, a threatening danger to our way of life, and an apparent potential for an invasion of this country. We have, I think, since awakened to the realities of the life-and-death struggle in which we are engaged with the Soviet Union. The launching of the Russian satellite has had one redeeming feature if nothing else: that of awakening the American public to the danger that surrounds them. To cope with this we are beginning, now, to revamp our educational structure. We are paying more attention to the mysteries of science, which we in our schools have not done previously. In the meantime our defense is being strengthened. Our knowledge in the field of astrophysics is being constantly improved with such experiments as will enable us to accelerate our momentum in our work in this field. I cannot help but believe that while we are behind the Russians in some phases of astrophysical development, there are many subjects in which we surpass them, and I do not feel that it will be too long a time before we are in a position to surpass them in those fields where we have permitted ourselves to decline.

It is quite apparent that there is no power on the face of the planet that possesses the will for conquest with the aggressive magnitude as that which is possessed by the present-day Russian Empire. Our world has not seen so grave a danger to its physical and moral existence since the fall of Rome; and the destruction of the Roman Empire plunged all of Europe into the Dark Ages. For, believe me, sir, if the Soviet Union and its satellites and allies triumph over the way of life as it is represented by the Western World, then just as assuredly shall our planet be forced by the circumstances to undergo another millennium of the Dark Ages.

April 16, 1958

My dear Colonel:

I was interested in your comment that General Norstadt has stated that the NATO countries must be armed with atomic weapons. I agree with him wholeheartedly, for if they are not, they will only be digging their own graves. By declining atomic weapons they would be leaving themselves wide open to Soviet aggression, and the Soviet Union would not hesitate in the slightest to use atomic weapons against any nation. The fact that the NATO nations would also have them would act as a deterrent against Soviet aggression—possibly not an extreme deterrent but sufficient to make the Soviets realize that their own troops and homeland would suffer a degree of devastation should they presume to attack the NATO countries. To me, a nation, refusing such weapons with which to defend itself while aware that the enemy nation would not hesitate to attack with his, is like an ostrich putting his head in the sand.

July 18, 1958

Dear Colonel:

I have been interested in the events that are taking place in the Middle East. Actually, what is happening, I think, is nothing less than a power play put into effect by Nasser of Egypt and supported by the Soviet Union.

We can only surmise the whys and the wherefores of the situation as it exists. Events are occurring with a staccato-like precision which tends to confuse the main issue: that of Arab nationalism. This expression means many things to many people. To Nasser it means the subversion of each individual Arabic entity to the single political entity of the Arab people. In accomplishing this the individual political unity of each Arabic nation is submerged and lost.

To the Western World Arab nationalism means the several Arabic political entities that make up the Middle East: that if there should be a unification of the political entities of the Arab world it should be on the basis of freedom of choice of the Arab people.

This play for power on the part of Nasser of Egypt has plunged the world into a ferment of turmoil, and behind it all stands the Soviet Union. Why?

I think the answer is relatively easy to ascertain if one will take the political history of Russia into account.

In the early years of the twentieth century when Nicholas II was the Czar of Russia the most ambitious foreign-policy program of the Russian government was the Pan-Slavic Movement. It never received its fruition during the Czarist regime, but it became an accomplished fact at the close of the Second World War. Russia, under the Soviet Government, achieved her ambition of becoming the dominant power in the Balkans. And while this was in progress there was also another sphere of unrest: the Middle East, where the Pan-Islamic Movement was gathering momentum. Here three of the world's greatest powers were vying for control: Great Britain, Russia, and Germany. As we know, the predominance of power in the Middle East fell to the British, with their control of that area and Suez.

By the end of the Second World War this power fell to the United States of America, a power which this nation used sparingly rather than aggressively.

In the meantime the dream of a Pan-Islamic unity was far from dead. The withdrawal of the British from the Middle East created a power vacuum in this area into which the United States failed to move with certainty and assurance. This created a reason for the existence of Nasser, and the dream of a Pan-Islamic Union with himself as the dominant and driving figure in such a move was promptly embraced by him.

But without the assistance of a powerful neighbor, Nasser is hardly in a position to fulfill his dream of Arab unity. It is here where the Russian play for power has begun. Russia's purpose, before the eyes of the world, is to act as a protecting father to Arab nationalism, but her main purpose is to become the dominant power in the eastern Mediterranean and the Middle East.

Concerning Arab nationalism, the American people couldn't care less, but it is for the purpose of thwarting Russian ambitions and designs in this part of the world that American and British troops have moved into Lebanon and Jordan respectively. And it was at the request of those governments that this was done.

What will eventually happen is difficult to say. It may result in a limited war such as took place in Korea. Actually, we do not know as yet. We must follow the sequence of events in order to ascertain what possibly might follow.

The Bay of Pigs debacle brought shame to many Americans who take pride in their country, and, possibly, to some who do not. It also brought a series of questions from some foreign observers, one, in particular, a priest in a small village in Yugoslavia. I had some difficulty in replying to him.

May 29, 1961

I must say that I and, I believe, a large number of my countrymen are both embarrassed and ashamed. I speak, of course, of the recent international events that have had serious political repercussions throughout our country. The Cuban debacle was completely unnecessary. The majority of our people (myself included) are sick and tired of that bearded psychopath who rules Cuba today. I firmly believe that when the invasion that was to overthrow the Communist regime in Cuba took place we should have gone in there with guns blazing, giving every tactical and strategic assistance to the Cuban rebels, even to the point of committing American Marines in that action. That we did not do so is a mistake. The political party that is in power in Washington is so afraid the South Americans would not like us if we were to do that. I frankly couldn't care less. I feel that when such a regime as that which is in Cuba has been permitted to come within ninety miles of our shores, then for our own future protection we should root it out, personally, if the other American nations show no interest in their protection.

Moreover, I am embarrassed and ashamed that our President is meeting with Khrushchev at this particular time. Nothing good can be accomplished by this meeting, and we will be embarrassed and humiliated again, just as we have been in the past. I, for one, am sick and tired of it, and I believe a majority of my countrymen are of the same opinion.

The latest outrage, however, is that our President has acquiesced to the blackmail scheme of Castro to send the Cubans tractors in return for twelve hundred Cuban prisoners he holds. I can well imagine what our Founding Fathers would say if they knew we had degenerated to this. It is the Barbary pirates and Tripoli all over again.

Fortunately, not all Americans are carved from this same stripe, and there is a wave of revulsion sweeping across the nation concerning it. The President is not supported in this at all. Fortunately, he cannot act in an official capacity in this matter and so commit the government to this folly. It must be done through private individuals, and these private individuals are endeavoring to raise the funds. I personally have no intention of giving one single penny toward this blackmail scheme. I hope others will not do so either, but I suppose there will always be some misguided fools who will.

All of this may sound a little harsh, and it probably is, but as one American, I have been pushed far enough by these people. I like peace, yes, but peace with honor and dignity. I don't want the peace of slavery. War is not to my liking. I have been through it and so have you, so we both know what it means. But I would rather die fighting than to be conquered piecemeal and do nothing to save my country.

Whether he be a PFC, a sergeant, a captain, or a general of the armies, whatever his rank, the American fighting man is supposed to be trained to be first class. Apparently, the Marine Corps follows this practice, for during the Vietnam War the corps turned out men who were really first rate. My correspondent was one of them.

September 2, 1965

Your letter arrived this morning. It was most interesting, and I was particularly intrigued with your story about the VC who tried to escape from the compound. It is really very simple. You are not behaving like a sadist at all, but what you felt is merely the reaction to your environment—a logical and natural reaction. If I had gone through what you have been going through I would react in the same manner. In fact, I do, even from here. When I think of what is happening to you boys in Vietnam and the viciousness of the enemy, even from here, I have no qualms whatsoever, about the type of revenge you may extract. With a Communist, and particularly an Asian Communist, the veneer of civilization is remarkably thin. They undoubtedly have never heard of the Hague Convention which regulated the rules of warfare. At any rate, they don't abide by them. Therefore, you cannot play the game by your rules. If you are to beat them you must put aside everything you have learned as regards fair play and beat them at their own game.

When you made the statement in your letter, "Before, if this had happened, it would have made me sick even to look at it. But now, it delighted me," you told me a great deal more about yourself then you realized. When that change took place you became a Marine. You didn't become a Marine when you were sworn in or when you went through boot camp. You became a Marine when that change of attitude took place. You're a first-class fighting man, Terry, and I'm proud of you.

February 8, 1969

Dear Terry:

Thank you for your letter, which arrived this morning. It was a pleasure to receive it, and it is a pleasure to know there are people like you still extant in the world today.

Many people wonder why you and your associates are in Vietnam at all. They say it is the wrong war in the wrong place at the wrong time. I am not one of them. You are in Vietnam now, associated with the Marine Corps in a military capacity, because of blunders that were made when decisions were rendered concerning various past military and diplomatic events. There are not many people who are aware of this, nor are they aware that we are today engaged in a Second Hundred Years War. As a nation we have been at war with the Communist philosophy since the year 1918, and with Russia for that length of time because that was when Communism became the official legacy of the Russian government.

We know that at that time Russia was in the throes of a revolution, a revolution so vast and terrible that it can only be likened to the French Revolution of 1793 in its horror. Like their French counterparts the Russian regicides brutally murdered Czar Nicholas II, the Czarina, and their family and threw their bodies down an abandoned salt mine in Ekaterinaberg, Siberia.

We know that Russia itself was not ready for the Communist Revolution, because the majority of the population were not oriented to its philosophy. So the Russian government, like the Chinese Communists forty years later, murdered approximately half a million Kulaks before effective opposition to their regime was finally crushed. Military opposition had already been suppressed.

From the point of view of its successful establishment in Russia the Communists began to export their revolutionary philosophy. It was almost successful in establishing itself in Germany after the First World War, and for a brief period of time, a Communist regime existed in Hungary, until it was overthrown a few months later. In those few months Hungary underwent the worst bloodbath in its history—including even the 1962 revolt, which came later.

The Communist battlefield was not in the cities or the open plains alone, or indeed in any other place where man fought against man in pitched battles. It was far more subtle than that. The Communists invaded the labor unions, the various branches of federal, state, and local governments, the classrooms in the high schools and colleges, where they not only spread their virus among the young and impressionable students but among the intellectual elite, the theoreticians among the university professors who, in the main, were disgruntled and dissatisfied with their economic lot because, up until a few years ago, a professor's pay was nothing worth noting. Today we are reaping the whirlwind on major high-school and university campuses.

But this war went on, and it was unlike any in the history of the world because it was not always a fighting war. It blew hot and cold by turns. That was the situation as it existed until September of 1929. Then, when a greater and more immediate menace arose and threatened the peace and security of the world powers, differences were set aside so that there might be a unification of forces to meet with and destroy a common enemy. The

Russians took full advantage of this, and thanks to an Allied second front, which held the German war machine in the West, the Russian armies swept through the Balkan countries of Eastern Europe and have been there ever since.

The American people, however, slumbered on, not yet aware of the dangers engendered by the Russian colossus and its philosophies. When, after the war was over, frantic aid was requested by the Nationalist Regime of China—which was fighting with its back against the wall against a Communist onslaught financed and supplied by the Russians—our nation, thanks to the pro-Communist element in the Department of State, saw to it that such aid, granted by Congress, never reached its destination, and Chiang-Kai-shek and his forces went down to defeat while the Department of State, in the words of Secretary of State Dean Atchison, was "waiting for the dust to settle."

For a while there was peace, such as there could be while the Chinese Communists consolidated their gains. Then came Korea and the first real military confrontation. The invasion of South Korea was met, as it should have been, by the forces of the United States, but they were not allowed to win the war because the political leaders of the time were fearful of a Russian entry into the conflict. This made the Communists bolder, and they expanded their view to Southeast Asia. There was a confrontation with the French in Vietnam, and the French were disastrously defeated. Vietnam was divided into two nations. The final confrontation began with the present war in Vietnam, in which again we are being forced, by the political leaders of our country, to sustain a "no win" policy on the battlefield. This is being enforced in the schools and colleges of our country by demonstrators who, to my mind, are traitors to our country.

If the Communists are permitted a political or military victory, either in Vietnam or at the negotiation table in Paris, it will mean the downfall of Southeast Asia and the withdrawal of the United States in its war against the Communists. There will be many more Vietnams unless we hold fast to where we are now. That, my friend, is the reason why those young soldiers of ours are where they are and why, in my admiration for them, I wish I were young enough to do more than just wish them Godspeed.

June 23, 1972

Dear Jim:

For a young man coming of age that period of time is always a complex one whether it be in the sixties, as you suggest, or earlier or later. I know it was for me. And you are correct when you say that many consider college a convenient continuation of high school. But difficult problems are not always easy to define. They never are. And since you mention it, the war in Vietnam is coming to a halt. But the United States, after making a commitment during the Kennedy years, and those of Johnson too, cannot unconditionally and immediately withdraw all of its forces. To do so would be to destroy not only the American prisoners of war but also the last remaining troops we have there while we were in the process of withdrawing them.

I must differ with you when you say that nearly seventy percent of our citizens want the war to end regardless of settlement. In my opinion the vast majority of the American people do care what the settlement is. I too believe we should withdraw, but not until our prisoners of war are returned and our commitments are fulfilled. I fully approve of what President Nixon has done as regards the war. Can you name any other president or senator who has done anything to get us out of the war? Fulbright, Kennedy, Bayh, McGovern—all of them have done everything in their power to sabotage the efforts of our country, and several of them have come close to treason.

The fact that McGovern stands a good chance of being nominated for the presidency scares me to death. That man implies he would be willing to go to Hanoi and surrender to the North Vietnamese by getting down on his knees and begging them to return our prisoners of war, and if those are his plans we will never get our prisoners of war back. Just imagine the spectacle of an American President-elect going to an enemy country to beg. That's what it amounts to. I am utterly appalled that that pinhead has gotten as far along toward the presidency as he has. He would lead the nation directly into moral bankruptcy.

A Final Prayer

In the Fall of 1976 I was greatly honored by the Optimist Club of Phoenix by being asked to give the Invocation at the Optimist Club of Phoenix Inaugural Banquet.

It would be fitting, I believe, to end this book with the same prayer.

Father in Heaven, we thank Thee for the many blessings Thou hast bestowed upon us.

On this evening of inauguration, when good friends are gathered together in harmony and fellowship, we give thanks for having had the benefit of the administration which is now coming to a close, and we thank Thee for the benefits which will accrue to us and to the youth of our community through the administration that is coming into office.

Use us, O Father, each through his own capacity, for Thy greater glory.

Bless and keep the youth of our nation in dignity and freedom; and may we, in our love for one another, find, through the Majesty of God, the Brotherhood of Man.